AF560653

KRISHNA'S CALL

KRISHNA'S CALL

Adi Kṛṣṇa Rama

Motilal Banarsidass Publications

MOTILAL BANARSIDASS
PUBLICATIONS
4741/23, Ansari Road, Daryaganj, New Delhi - 110002 (India)
Email: mlbd@mlbd.com | sales@mlbd.com | exports@mlbd.com
Website: www.mlbd.com

Krishna's Call
by
Adi Kṛṣṇa Rama

First Edition Published in 2024

Published in India by Motilal Banarsidass Publications

ISBN : 978-81-96165-37-6 (HB)

Printed and bound in India

Foreword

To me, Bhagavad Gita, the Song of the Divine, is an ancient gem that shines eternally and becomes more and more radiant and relevant for the whole of humanity. It is more than a scripture; it is a divine dialogue between an enlightened master, Krishna, and his beloved friend Arjuna, who becomes his devotee during this process when he becomes capable of witnessing the incarnation of superconsciousness in front of him. This very process unfolds the dance of existence and its enigmatic beauty.

Krishna, the timeless maestro, bestowed a vision of humanity beyond duality, transcending the binds of mundane existence and the escape of the renunciate. Yet, over millennia, this vision grew dim, and we found ourselves in the throes of subjugation. But the spirit of Bharat, once subdued, was destined to rise again. Swami Vivekananda, Sri Aurobindo, Mahatma Gandhi—these were the visionaries that began the resurgence, the awakening of a nation's soul. And in the wake of independence, the legacies of Maharishi Ramana, Jiddu Krishnamurti, and my beloved master, Osho, have carried the torch, illuminating the path forward.

Today, Swami Rama extends the invitation through these pages, reaching out to those ready to embark on the sacred, ancient journey. I trust that this book will spark a revolution in consciousness, akin to the awakening Krishna envisioned for Arjuna, ensuring that our cherished Bharat will once more emerge as a beacon of peace, prosperity, and profound wisdom.

I have known swamiji for many years—with deep silence of meditation pulsing at his core and melodies of flute gracing his heart, embodying the witnessing consciousness and playful spirit that Osho spoke of as the essence of a sadhak and a true devotee. Only through such depth of devotion, one is an instrument of the divine infinite and a true master.

"Life is the only shrine of existence, and to be playful about it is the only prayer." OSHO, on Leela (divine play).

Embrace this book as your confidant, your beacon of light. Swamiji's words are crafted to cleave through life's entanglements and illuminate the trails where challenges abound. These are not just the words of the Gita but a call for the emergence of the 'New Human.' May this rendition of the Bhagavad Gita inspire you to step into the boundless potential that awaits within.

Swami Chaitanya Keerti

Author's Note

Beloved Ones,

Life is a celebration, a dance of existence, and amidst this vast play, there lies a scripture, the Bhagavad Gita, which sings the very song of the cosmos.

Have you ever felt its presence? As you embark on your inner journey, the Bhagavad Gita mysteriously finds its way to you. It shines as a guiding light, becomes a friend in solitude, and offers solace in moments of despair. Swami Vivekananda recognized this eternal companion, naming it the "divine mother."

My own communion with Krishna's song was kindled by an unexpected source during my childhood—Stephen Hawking's "A Brief History of Time." Within the complex interplay of science, amidst dialogues about black holes and relativity, I met the boundless—the infinite. The mind, constrained by its very design, hesitates at the threshold of infinity, and thought is incapable of conceiving it, even through imagination. Yet the heart dares to dive deep, to merge, to unify with this profound vastness.

During this silent union, the Bhagavad Gita manifested as a living presence for me, a maternal embrace, guiding and bestowing upon me infinite love and wisdom.

The Bhagavad Gita isn't just a book; it's the universe voicing itself. It's a harmonious blend of science, poetry, and philosophy. It captures the essence of our ancient Bharat, steering souls towards luminosity and love. For me, it's a meditation, a tender whisper from the divine to the yearning spirit.

Through this modest offering, I've strived to convey the Gita's essence in contemporary language, yet its spirit remains eternal. Immerse yourself in it. Let it transcend mere reading, evolving into an experience, a metamorphosis, a profound inner voyage towards your very core.

May this book enlighten and inspire you. Whether you journey through it chapter by chapter or seek guidance by spontaneously opening any page, may it be a beacon for your path.

With love and blessings.

Introduction

Om Namo Bhagavate Vāsudevāya

In the vast tapestry of Vedic wisdom, the Bhagavad Gita shines brightly as a beacon of spiritual insight and practical guidance. The timeless dialogue between Lord Krishna and Arjuna is not just a conversation on the battlefield, but a profound introspection on life, purpose, and the eternal quest for self-realisation. This work endeavours to extract the essence of the Bhagavad Gita, chapter by chapter, not in a verbatim recount, but as a distillation of its profound truths, aiming to make them accessible and relatable to the contemporary seeker in a language that is easy to understand.

Often, when it is mentioned "Krishna says," it is not a literal citation, but a representation of the underlying principles, ideas, and lessons conveyed by Him. This approach has been adopted to emphasize the universality of the wisdom imparted, rather than its literary specifics.

In the pursuit of understanding the Gita, the book draws upon the vast reserves of other ancient scriptures, such as the Upanishads and the Brahman Sutras. These texts, in their own right, have explored profound depths of spirituality and philosophy, complementing the Gita's teachings and offering additional layers of comprehension.

This commentary is an invitation—a call to dive deep into the ocean of Vedic wisdom. It is designed for both the novice, curious about the foundations of Indian philosophy, and the seasoned seeker, looking for a fresh perspective. By threading the pearls of ancient wisdom with a contemporary thread, this book hopes to bridge millennia of spiritual teaching and modern-day understanding.May the journey through these pages bring you closer to the eternal wisdom of the Gita and closer to your own inner Self.

About the Author

Om Namo Bhagavate Vāsudevāya

Swami Adi Rama's journey is one that bridges worlds. From the silent majesty of the Himalayas, where he immersed himself in the depths of ancient teachings, to the bustling corridors of modern leadership in business, politics and administration, Guruji has touched the soul of both eras.

His heart has been trained by the Himalayas, ancient and contemporary enlightened masters, and by the melodious wisdom flowing from his flute, a gift nurtured under the guidance of the legendary Pandit Hari Prasad Chaurasia.

More than a guide, Swami Rama is a companion for those seeking. He has guided the ancient secrets to leaders and dreamers, illuminating their paths. His course, "The Art of Decisions for Leaders" is not just about making choices and achieving success; it is about making a difference, finding meaning and living fully.

In this book, he extends his hand to you. With each page, he beckons you closer to the timeless wisdom of the Bhagavad Gita, sharing its warmth, its guidance, its heart. It is more than just words—it's a heart-to-heart conversation across time.

Connect with Adi Kṛṣṇa Rama on Instagram:
www.instagram.com/AdiKrsnaRama

Contents

Overview of the Chapters

Chapter 1 explains the context of Bhagavad Gita. The reader is introduced Arjun's dilemma of having to fight his own family and friends, and Krishna takes on the responsibility of guiding Arjuna through this.

Chapter 2 points the attention inside, towards Ātman, our eternal self. The reader is guided to follow svadharma, where total action in devotion becomes as a way to inner realisation.

Chapter 3 delves into the paths of jnana yoga and karma yoga. Yajña, the action of dharma in awakened mindfulness is the way, neither inaction or blind action.

Chapter 4 explains how Ātman manifests as Krishna in the world. The reader is guided to aim for inner realisation to be freed from the cycle of rebirth and have a choice. It gives an understanding of actions and shows how yajña and mastery of body, mind and prana is the way forward.

Chapter 5 establishes the interconnectedness between jnana yoga and karma yoga, and Krishna presents a simplified version of karma yoga as devoting your actions to the divine. The chapter urges shifting between self-enquiry and mastery of emotions, body and prana, and it concludes with a powerful meditation technique for seeing the seer within.

Chapter 6 describes the state of equanimity of the enlightened being and guides the reader onto the royal path of Krishna that will benefit your life tremendously even if you only follow it partially. Krishna explains an ancient meditation technique for inner liberation.

Chapter 7 establishes bhakti or devotion as the key to all yogas. It is an invitation to be in love with the divine, know the divine and merge into it. Krishna depicts Maya as the manifestation of the three gunas or inner natures and urges the reader to aim for sattva and beyond.

Chapter 8 explores transcendence of death and provides guidance for the moment of death. The crux of the teaching is remembrance. It describes the nine expressions of bhakti and introduces the way of seeing everything as Brahman or divine.

Chapter 9 explains the law of karma and how to be free of it through self-realisation, dissolving in Ishvara through devotion. It guides the reader to the raj yoga, the path of devotion and consciousness.

Chapter 10 focuses on remembrance as the key to liberation and transcendence of death through anchoring your mind in Krishna and devoting every moment to him. It explores the importance of excellence as a way of being close to the divine.

Chapter 11 shifts our perspective to the infinite existence and instructs the reader to aim for the divine and not be limited by identification with the life stories.

Chapter 12 clarifies whether to worship the form or formless. Krishna provides practical suggestions for overcoming challenges on the different paths of yoga, and the reader is guided to develop compassion and achieve a state of equanimity through mastering emotions.

Chapter 13 emphasises the maxim "know thyself." It suggests that the self that must be understood is the non-die self, a concept that paves the way for the understanding of the Ishvara principle.

Chapter 14 delves into mastering the three gunas: sattva, rajas, and tamas. The reader is urged to take control of their life through mastering the gunas, developing their own goals and values and cultivate good habits.

Chapter 15 details how to become free from birth, death and rebirth through either devotion or renunciation of inner identification. It gives detailed instruction on enlightenment in the moment of death. The crux of the teachings is remembrance of the divine.

Chapter 16 provides the basic understandings needed for the spiritual journey. It explores the inner qualities that are crucial to develop and points out traits that will hinder reaching the divine.

Chapter 17 explores the three gunas' effect on our worship, food habits and sharing and guides the reader to bring these important areas towards sattva. The chapter concludes with an introduction to the potent mantra Om Tat Sat.

Chapter 18 explains how the inner paths are interconnected and advises to be true to your inner nature. It guides the reader how to come out of the comfort zone of the tamas state, how to overcome the challenges of rajas and reach sativa and the divine beyond.

Chapter 1

Amidst the Din of War, a Warrior's Heart Quivers

On each side of the big battle ground, two mighty armies stand ready for battle. All the 100 Kaurava princes with their huge and powerful army on one side against the five Pandavas princes and their much smaller army. Among the Pandavas is Arjuna, a warrior unrivalled in archery, and along with him is the great Lord Krishna who has taken the role of charioteer and guide of Arjuna. On the side of the Kauravas is prince Suyodhana, later called Duryodhana, who is the leader of the Kauravas and propagator of the war. The Kauravas are supported by Karana, the greatest warrior ever, the finest and bravest and son of Surya the sun god. Along with the Kauravas is Guru Drona, the martial arts trainer of both the Pandavas and Kauravas. The Kauravas are also supported by Bhishma, the great-grandfather and guide to the kingdom, along with Krishna's own army of courageous and brave warriors.

On the side of the Pandavas, Krishna and Arjuna are standing on their rath or chariot. Their flag carrying sri Hanuman is blowing from the top of the rath. Everyone has put their shankhanad, their battle cry, and now there is no way back. The armies are ready, and the battle is about to begin.

The first chapter of the Gita is on the call of the battle. The modern times has its own battles. There is a call of battle in everyday life, when you wake up in the morning to go to your shop to do business, when as a mother you start the day ready to deal with kids and house chores, when you as a leader sit down at your desk that is full of problems you have to deal with. This is the call of the battle in everyday life in the modern day, but in the ancient times it was a real battle.

Exactly after putting the cry of the battle Arjuna drops his weapon and asks, Krishna, how can I fight? How it is possible for me to fight? These are my brothers, how can I fight them? What is the point of fighting and why should I fight? These are the questions in Arjuna's mind.

If you do not know the Mahabharata, Arjuna may appear weak in dropping his weapons and not wanting to fight. But knowing the full story of Mahabharata we see that Arjuna is both brave and strong.

Now Arjuna has asked a very relevant question. If Arjuna were not asking this, we should be worried because that would mean a non-empathetic person was on that side, someone going to battle without considering the consequences of his actions. But no, Arjuna is sensitive. He asks, would it not be better that I do not fight? Would it not be better if I let them kill me, let myself be slaughtered? Then at least I would be known as someone who stood with peace. What is the point of fighting? These are Arjun's questions to Krishna. And the state Arjuna is in should be one's state when going to battle, because if you are going to battle for blood there is something wrong, if you are not feeling like Arjuna, questioning the point of the battle.

In the context of modern day, it would be asking yourself, what is the point of repetitive tasks every day? What is the point of doing the same things over and over, repeating day after day after day? Doing business and fighting for profit, what is the point?

Asking this question shows sincerity, honesty and clarity in Arjun's heart. It shows a deep longing to know the truth and a broken heart. He is asking the question, why?

This is where Krishna is taking on the responsibility of guide, putting flute away and taking command of the horses to lead Arjuna into battle. This tells something about Krishna. He puts aside his flute, takes command of the horses, points in the direction of the battlefield, looks at Arjuna and answers his questions and inquiries. This is where we move to chapter two.

Chapter 2

In Whispers of the Cosmos, Truth Begins to Rise

In this chapter Arjuna is in sorrow. His heart is broken and he is perplexed. With his feet on the ground and his bow in the sand, he looks at Krishna and asks, what do I do? All my friends and family are on the other side of the battleground. Now what do I do?

Arjuna might have expected an answer of peace from Krishna, the great warrior who has been known to always aim for peace. He might have expected him to say, yes, why should one fight? If you read Bhagavad Gita without the bigger context of Mahabharata, the story before and after Bhagavad Gita, it may appear that Krishna is proposing war, but that is completely untrue. When you know Mahabharata, you realise that Krishna was the greatest supporter of peace. He is even called "the one who runs away from battles". In the previous parts of Mahabharata, we see that Krishna tried to negotiate peace many times. Nobody worked as hard for peace as Krishna. He met everybody from both the sides.

In one person he met arrogance and in another ignorance, in one the attitude was "blood for blood" and in another helplessness and giving up. This is the story of Krishna, he is full heartedly supporting peace.

Krishna now looks at Arjuna and says, it is heartbreaking to see you like this, my dear brother. I will show you the path. First he motivates him by calling him a great warrior and then he guides him.

Krishna tells Arjuna about **Ātman.** In modern times Ātman is misunderstood as some kind of spirit in the body, but here Krishna clearly describes Ātman saying, Ātman is that which cannot be burned by fire, which cannot be cut by sword, which cannot be moved by anything, which cannot be touched by neither thought nor emotion. Krishna is making Arjuna aware of this inner state of being which is beyond sorrow, which is beyond any human emotion and yet is fully awake, fully alive, fully sensitive and fully present.

In this moment, Krishna is very aware of Arjuna's emotional state and state of being, so he is giving this knowledge very gently. He is telling Arjuna to see Ātman in himself. See that which cannot be touched by anything, neither thought, nor emotion and neither senses nor experience can reach.

Through his guidance Krishna is showing Arjuna the path of vedanta, the path to know his true self, to know the nature of reality. Vid means to see, vidya is to know through seeing, ved is manifestation of the knowing and vedanta is the peak of knowing. Bhagavad Gita is the peak of vedanta, the peak of all the knowledge which comes from seeing.

As Krishna speaks about Ātman, he also mentions that the body is bound to die one day. It is born, and it will pass. No matter what thought, what feeling, what emotion you are facing, that shall too pass. And what remains is Ātman.

Now, the mind would like to create an image of Ātman, that Ātman is a soul, like a spirit that lives in us. That is a misconception one could derive, but Krishna does not say that anywhere. What Krishna says is, Ātman is that which cannot be burned by fire, which cannot be cut by sword, which no emotion can touch, which no thought can reach, and no experience can know. This is Ātman.

Know that Ātman is your true nature, that which has never been born and will never die, that which has no beginning and no end. Krishna is describing an alive infinite within ourselves. An alive infinite, living through this Nashwar Sharir, this mortal body which is sooner or later bound to die, the senses which dulls with the age and eventually fades away and finishes.

Krishna is pointing his arrow inwards, toward Dharmakṣetra. Where Arjuna is looking outwards to the battlefield, the Kurukṣetra, Krishna is pointing his attention inwards. This is the core message of the second chapter of Bhagavadgītā, not only to look outwards, towards outer achievements, towards actions and decisions, towards the material success you are seeking or towards aims and ambitions. Do not focus only on the outer battlefield. Look inwards, and keep looking inwards until you reach Ātman. Do not stop at the body, do not stop at the senses, do not stop at the emotions, do not stop at the feelings, do not stop at the thoughts, do not stop at observer, the one observing everything, your so called self which is created by the history and education system, by your experiences and your conditionings. Do not stop at that. Do not stop until you reach your true self. It is divine, it is an absolute reflection of the divine. Until you reach there do not stop, do not settle, do not compromise, do not settle for mediocrity, go to the very core of your being and you will discover Ātman. This is exactly what Krishna is showing

Arjuna. In the ups and downs of Kurukṣetra do not forget Dharmakshetra, from where you and your Kurukṣetra are born and eventually will dissolve.

After pointing out this, after describing the nature of reality, Krishna makes Arjuna aware of his **svadharma**, of his dharma, his duty, what he needs to do. Krishna motivates him saying, do your duty, do your dharma, because this is who you are. It is natural that he is a warrior. He is trained to be a warrior, that is his core nature. In this part Krishna is reminding him of that saying, this is who you are.

When you do your action full heartedly, with total devotion, with total surrender to the action, then the path to Ātman becomes very easy and direct. And the moment you see Ātman in yourself, you will see it in others. The core of your life becomes a manifestation of Ātman, a manifestation of Paramātman. Your action becomes a manifestation of divine itself.

This is the direction Krishna is showing Arjuna. He is pointing to the path of dharma, the path of svadharma. He is advising to be true to the meaning and purpose you derive from your action, to be true to the flow of your action and to be true to the nature of reality and the insights that come through the flow of your action. This is the essence of Krishna's guidance.

First Krishna tells to point your attention inwards, then he illuminates the impermanent nature of the senses, the body, the mind, the thought and everything. He says, when you point your focus inwards, it is your dharma, the path of your action, which will take you to Ātman. Krishna does not say just meditate to find Ātman. He says, wherever you are, whatever action you are doing, be total in it, be complete in it. That complete action will guide you, will show you the path to Ātman. And Ātman is Paramātman, the divine, the alive infinite. Usually the mind gives excuses like, "I need to find Paramātman, I need to find enlightenment", but Krishna does not leave any room for excuses. He says, devote yourself to your dhanush, your bow and arrow that you put on the ground. Devote yourself to your action. Devote yourself to the flow of the action, to the purpose and the meaning you derive from it. This will guide you to Ātman.

The moment you see Ātman in yourself, you see it in the other also. It becomes your reality, it becomes the nature of your being.

Be brave, stand up and rise to the challenge. Rise. Know fearlessness, know courage, know action.

With this beautiful insight Krishna is guiding Arjuna saying, dear Arjuna, this is your path. When you know Ātman, your mind becomes calm, your mind becomes sthira or stable and you see clearly. The thought becomes clear and the fog of emotions disappears.

The state Krishna describes is the state of awakening, the state of enlightenment. What Krishna describes is bound to happen when you discover your true self. You will be able to master your senses, you will be able to master your conditionings, you will be the master of your actions.

This is a knowing and the path goes towards understanding this knowledge, getting to see yourself as Ātman - not believing yourself as Ātman but seeing it. Reaching there, your mind is stable, calm and clear. There is a natural insight and flow of life, a continuous flow of life through you. And from that space, whatever action you take, that action is in alignment with the existence.

So rise up and fight. Follow your dharma. Be brave, be

fearless, be courageous. Be true to the meaning and purpose you derive from your action. See the nature of reality as it is. Seek that higher state of being and know it. It can be known now, this very moment, not out there in the future, wherever you are, through your duty, through your action.

This is chapter two, one of the finest guides to enlightenment which leaves no room for excuses, which is not shying away from responsibilities but being total in your action with knowing the nature of the reality.

Vid, Vidya, Ved, Vedanta. The path to jnana yoga, the path to karma yoga.

Chapter 3

Graceful Flow, Destiny's Path Reverses

In this chapter Arjuna is confused. One of the things I love about Arjuna is that however he feels, he has the courage and honesty to say it. And he knows how he feels, he pays attention. Arjuna says, oh Krishna, your words are confusing me. If you say that jnana, the path of vedanta is higher than anything else, then why are you asking me to go to battle? Why are you asking me to fight? Should I not rather meditate and point my attention inwards to Ātman and find out who I am? What is this? I am confused. You have confused me totally.

Krishna being Krishna, he smiles. He smiles and says, my dear Arjuna, I understand your confusion. I understand what you are going through, and I see that it is difficult.

He then explains that it is not by inaction, by just meditating and enquiring "who am I?", that you will reach. Neither will you reach by blindly indulging in action as the rest of the world. It is not that simple.

Arjuna replies that, if this is not the case, then please guide me to the path of blessedness, this state of Ātman, which is Paramātman, which is enlightenment. Please show me the path.

Now Krishna shows Arjuna **the path of awakening**, of blessedness, of Buddha nature, the path of enlightenment and liberation. Throughout human history it has had many different names.

Krishna says, the path is through knowing, through jnana, but be aware, nothing in this universe goes without action. I, the manifestation of divine itself, I am here with you in the battlefield, fighting alongside you. There is no such action prescribed for me in this universe and yet I am here with you. Know that you cannot go without action. This is the essence of Krishna's guidance.

The yogis or monks who try without action, their mind is in illusion by the senses, by desire and by laziness. Their own mind is leading them astray. Know that it is not possible, it is a delusion to go into inaction in order to achieve enlightenment. The path you are thinking of does not lead anywhere. It is a dead end.

Why does Krishna say it is a dead end? Because in inaction the mind would be busy with the same desires and the same objects of gratification. What you want would be bothering you. And then laziness would take over and dull your senses, so neither you would have your desires fulfilled nor you would do your actions. You would be in a pretty sad state.

Now Krishna moves on to show **the path of action**, the path of karma yoga. He says that neither inaction will take you to Ātman, nor will blind action which almost the whole humanity is busy with. It is **yajña**, the highest form of action that will take you there. Yajña has several meanings. One meaning is of the vedic yajña where you put herbs and ghee into the fire and chant mantras. Krishna is talking about yajña in the original meaning of following your dharma. This yajña is when you derive meaning and purpose from your action, when the flow of energy is harmonious, when you are in a deep flow and you are in a state of samadhi. The rest of the world disappears and only oneness with action remains. In that state you are not motivated by ambition, by greed, by fear or by the fruit of your action. The action in this state happens naturally, as a manifestation, as a flow.

Sports people call this state being in the zone, when they are playing and they are fully there in the action and nothing else remains. For a tennis player just the ball and the tennis remains, the rest of the world disappears. Arjuna describes a glimpse of the state of yajña earlier in Mahabharata, when he said, I see nothing but my target and my bow and arrow. At that moment he is in a state of samadhi, a state of meditation. This is the yajña Krishna is pointing towards as flow of life. The action being done in this state is the action to liberation. Aim for that state of being when you are in action.

Yajña comes from finding meaning and purpose in your actions, or from giving your actions purpose and meaning. In motherhood, mothering is an action and the mother's full dedication to motherhood is her action. In that action, when she is fully dedicated, fully devoted, that action itself becomes a source of energy and the being flowers and there is a transformation in life.

Follow your **dharma**, do the right thing, do your duty and find meaning in your duty. Find your **svadharma**, find passion, purpose, meaning in your action.

Actions can have many expressions, like the action of thought or thinking, the action of decision making and physical actions. For the body there is a duty to keep it healthy, fit and fine by giving it the right diet and the right exercise. For the mind there is a duty to keep it sharp by giving it all the knowledge and necessary means it requires to be able to think clearly. There is a duty towards your inner space to keep it free of fear, greed and blind ambition, to have a clarity of feeling, a deep feeling of love, compassion, mindfulness and awareness. Then there is the action for manifesting abundance and prosperity in your life. Which action could bring you that? Which action could make you win over poverty and ill health? These are duties to yourself. Find the actions needed to fulfil those duties.

Find the actions which are in alignment with your passion, with the expression of who you are as a person. This is what Krishna calls svadharma. It is your duty to yourself to find it and be committed to it.

What is your duty to society, what is your action? Everything is interconnected, Krishna says. There is a natural harmony in this universe. If you are a soldier, if you are a warrior, then stay true to it. Do not judge it as being higher or lower, because without you this natural harmony would not be there.

Do the right thing, as Krishna describes, but do it as a yajña. If you do it without yajña, without being in the zone, being in the flow, the natural state of samadhi, awakened samadhi or mindfulness, flow and awareness in your action, then your action is equal to inaction. So neither fall into the trap of inaction nor the trap of action without the flow of yajña. Do the yajña. Convert every action during the day into yajña, and yajña will take you to transformation.

Now Krishna goes on to describe **jnana** in a deeper way, showing the way Maharishi Ramana calls, "who am I", finding out who you are. Do not be deluded that you are your body, that you are your senses, that you are your thoughts, your desires, your ambitions. All of this is part of life and they are life, but do not be deluded that you are that only. See diligently that you are not this, not that either, not this, not this, not this. Keep going deeper and deeper in this way, seeing and knowing.

Continuing like this there will come a point where you see that only the observer remains and nothing else. You observe, and in that observer, see the observer itself. Know the knower, as Vedanta expresses it. Witnessing the witness, as Osho says. See the seer, as the ancient scriptures describes it.

When in action ask yourself, who is doing this action? Ask that question, see that question. Who am I? Who am I?

Continuing this enquiry with full intensity and urgency, there comes a point where the seer is seen, and the state of non-duality prevails.

Start with seeing how the I is created by the conditioned personality, the conditioned thoughts, body, mind and emotions. This is what creates your sense of I. Do not be deluded by it. See how this I, which you call yourself, is formed, and do not be limited by it. Know the Ātman, Krishna says. By knowing the Ātman you know the Paramātman. Krishna describes it as Ātman, but even if we give no description, that would be a description in itself. Saying not this, not that is another way to describe it.

Krishna says, know the path of jnana. He does not say either or, either jnana or karma. To Arjuna he says, both ways are yours. The separation of these two ways into separate paths is a misunderstanding. People say, "I am on the jnana path" or "I am on the karma yog path". Krishna does not say anywhere that these are separate paths, he says that they are intertwined. If you know yajña, then karma will take you to jnana, and if you know jnana, it will give you the insight of doing the right thing.

Krishna says, I am the blessed one, yet I am doing the duty, yet I am in the world, yet I am playing flute, yet I am in the battlefield fighting alongside you as your charioteer and guide.

In this way Krishna clears the misunderstanding of the separate paths. He is guiding Arjuna to the next level, to the deeper aspects of Samadhi, of blessedness.

After this, Krishna gives a short introduction to the gunas, the three different energies or natures which he will describe in much more detail in the later chapters. Here he says, rajas gives you the desire to achieve, to know and to reach. That energy is there in you and it is fine. Live it, it is your svabhav, your character. But also know that yajña is beyond that, and your path is towards yajña. Live rajas, but eventually merge into yajña.

Master the gunas and yajña will become effortless. Through the mastery of gunas the path of action, karma yoga becomes effortless and it becomes divine. So master yourself through knowing, through seeing, through the divine knowledge.

Chapter 4

Love's Silent Call, an Eternal River

Before starting on chapter 4, there is something that we must understand. Krishna does not speak to Arjuna as a student, neither as a disciple. He talks to him as a devotee. Devotee? Who is a devotee? A devotee is someone deeply in love and totally surrendered. The heart of the devotee is leading, not the ego, mind or thought. With the student, the mind is leading, he wants to learn. But Krishna says, my devotee. A devotee is totally surrendered, in love, open and receiving.

Krishna also calls Arjuna brother and friend. This is unique. We are talking about the greatest guru that ever existed, but he does not appear like a guru at all. He is in the battle field wearing armour, taking the role of Arjun's charioteer. He plays flute and dances. He is a completely different human being. He does not look like one imagines a guru would look. That is the illusion. That is why he did not attract many students or disciples at his time. Today, everybody respects the great Lord Krishna. But in his own time, it was Arjuna who walked along with him.

It is Arjun's bravery, courage, devotional heart and friendship that Krishna loves, and these qualities is what makes Arjuna capable of receiving this knowledge. But why does Krishna say, you are receiving this knowledge? To learn and to receive, these are two completely different ways. Between a guru and disciple there is a flow, a transmission of light, like when you put a lit candle close to another, the flame transmits and lights the other candle. This is reception. Learning is gathering knowledge. Sometimes it lays a foundation for receiving but often not.

Listen to the story of the five pots. Three of the pots represent an attitude that prevents us from fully receiving in life. The first pot is filled to the brim, like someone so full of knowledge, ideas and opinions that there is no room left for anything new. The second pot is filled with poison, like someone with poisonous ideas of own superiority, entitlement, lack of feeling and empathy. Whatever that person will receive will be poisoned and used for furthering the ego. The third pot with a hole is like a distracted person where the body is present but the thoughts and attention are elsewhere. The rise of mobile phones has created many such holes in the modern mind. Nothing stays in it. Unlike the three first pots the fourth pot is empty, like the disciple, ready to receive. The fifth pot is also empty, but it is made of different clay, of the longing for the divine, surrender and courage, like a devotee. Like Arjuna.

Now Krishna says, this is the teaching I gave to Sūrya and many before and after. He describes how he imparted this knowledge to many of the Raja Rishis, the great Rishis. And now he is giving this knowledge to Arjuna.

Arjuna says, I understand. But I am confused. You are here so how could you teach them?

This question is typical of Arjuna. He just believes what he sees. He is not a visionary or a great thinker, he is just asking a very simple question. And it is a good question. I see you in the physical form, so how could it be possible?

Krishna then explains how the body is mere clothes and the mind is merely an expression of Ātman. As I mentioned earlier there is a common misunderstanding of Ātman being some form of spirit or energy which leaves the body. But this is not what Krishna describes and neither is it the reality. Ātman does not go anywhere. It is the body which drops. Would you say that you left your clothes? Or did the clothes drop and you wore new clothes?

The **manifestation of Ātman** in the body happens through the desire to be born again, through the desire to live and experience again or through the momentum of karmic impressions which have been building over a period of time in the sphere of the mind.

In order to truly understand this, we need to go to the ancient wisdom of Sāṃkhya. Sāṃkhya describes the cosmic presence, Ishvara. From this cosmic presence the cosmic life and cosmic mind emerges. The cosmic mind expresses itself in form of evolution of individual life forms and later, with the human beings and the blessing of a growing consciousness, the separation grows as the self is formed and the consciousness is limited to the self and the self's experiences of itself in form I, me, my etc. Hence the illusion of separation from the cosmic presence, Ātman. And this consciousness of the self is often confused as soul.

This self, this illusion of separation gathers experiences and karmas. Over a period of time it gathers many desires and sufferings, both material and spiritual. Hence the cycle of birth and rebirth.

After explaining this, Krishna steps back and says, this is how the birth and rebirth happen, but I am free from the cycle of birth and rebirth. And yet, whenever the **dharma** is in trouble I manifest.

One could be confused as to the meaning of dharma here. See, at that time the Kauravas were acting like they did not care about anything but themselves. Duryodhana was acquiring more and more at any cost. He knew that there was a battle coming, that there was a war on the way and many people would die. His own people would die. But he still did not care. He just kept on going at whatever cost.

What was happening at that time? There was such a deep ignorance and mind without consciousness, such egoistic behaviour continuing endlessly, that it became impossible for consciousness to grow into the values of spirituality, of compassion, of different yogas, of devotion, of jnana, of different yagyas. The collective mind, which is collected experiences of the self over thousands of years, had started coming in the way of flowering of consciousness.

The individual is where consciousness can flower as strength of clarity through jnana, as passion, purpose and meaning through karma and devotion, as heart and consciousness flowering in form of art, culture, beauty and nature. All this suffers due to the powerful collective mind. So know that divine sees the potential in you and takes care of you.

Krishna says, I manifest. This is not Krishna as a personal manifestation. It is Atman's direct manifestation without the elusive self.

Then Krishna explains that Ishvara consciousness is available to all, at all times. The path to blessedness, to awakening, nirvana, or enlightenment as it has been called in more recent times, this path is available to all.

Krishna says, after enlightenment happens, there is no rebirth. There is manifestation. You can reincarnate and rebirth is your choice. It becomes a choice for you rather than an endless, continuous **cycle of birth and rebirth**, reiterating the same over and over again.

See it for yourself. It requires almost 20 to 25 years for us to be independent. And by the time we figure out that our life will not last forever, old age is already knocking on the door. The life is a pretty short affair. And it is a repetitive affair without much freedom, because you are bound by where you are born, by what education you get and who your parents are, which is manly random or karmic and without any choice on your part.

What Krishna says is, aim for freedom so you can have a choice. You can still be reborn, but with a choice. You do have a choice. You can reincarnate if you choose to. But you would not have any desire for reincarnation unless there is a very strong compassion or an intense love for inner freedom. Then you may come back in order to give this choice or this freedom to the world. Then that will bring you back for the good of the humanity.

See that the cycle of birth and rebirth is the same phenomenon repeating again and again. It is like a kid addicted to video games. The kid is playing the same video game on repeat, but the urge to play it one more time remains. The parent can see it from the outside and asks, "what are you busy with?" And if the parent tells the kid that he can be free from playing the game on repeat, the kid would answer, "why would I want to be free from it?" The parent is trying is to create a choice by saying, "look, step back from the game for some time. You can still go back and play if you want to spend some time with your friends while playing it. That is still possible." But the kid says, "you are asking me to come out of it."

There is a widespread misconception that moksha or liberation is permanently closing the door to the world. Why would we want to do that? But moksha is freedom from addiction to the repetitive game. Moksha gives you that freedom. And here Krishna is telling Arjuna, look, this is available to you. You do not need to stay bound. You do not need to keep reiterating without realising it. Do not be in that game. Do not be the kid addicted to video game or the young teenager addicted to social media without seeing the issue in it. Step back. It is possible to step back from it. You can create freedom for yourself. And not only for yourself, you can create that freedom for others also, as Krishna does. He is setting an example by his actions. What a blessing Arjuna received, being at the feet of the master of masters and getting drenched in the divine song of wisdom.

In the movie Matrix, Morpheus gives Neo a choice. Take the blue pill and you will see you the truth or take the red pill and stay in the contended experience of ordinary reality. It is a very interesting moment. An even deeper phenomenon than this is taking place in Mahabharata where Krishna explains that you have a choice.

Now Arjuna starts to understand. I see, my dear brother, he says, my guru, my master, manifestation of the divine. I see you, I hear, Krishna. Arjuna start to see this and he asks, how?

Krishna then takes Arjuna to **understanding of action**. What is action? What different expressions of actions are there? And how can one be attached to one's action and create the doer in the process? This is the direction Krishna is leading Arjuna.

In order to fully understand what Krishna is talking about here, one must go to Sāṃkhya, which is a foundation. Unfortunately most of the scriptures of Sāṃkhya were destroyed during the last thousand years, and it has become a lost art. We have scriptures from Vedanta. We have scriptures from Tantra. We have Agamas. We have scriptures from Buddhist. We have scriptures from the school of Nyaya Niti and Vaisheshika. But Sāṃkhya scriptures somehow disappeared, and we have only one or two scriptures. One is by Ishvara Krishna. And some parts of the Kapilamuni scriptures are there. Gita is the only other place where we find some of the understandings of Sāṃkhya.

Krishna's guru, rishi Sandipani, with whom he studied, was dedicated to Sāṃkhya, Vedanta and yoga, and of these Sāṃkhya was the preparatory part.

Sāṃkhya is too vast to explain here, but to give a short introduction, it is the science of how the formation of our mind, buddhi and ego takes place. Sāṃkhya describes the formation of the gunas, the different kinds of nature, how the gunas are established through our senses. It describes how we experience our senses and how the attention and awareness moves.

Now, Krishna says, when you are doing an action, any kind of action, if that action is not complete, not total, then that action is bound to **create the doer**. That action is bound to create attachment either with the action, with the result of the action or with the doer. If not attachment, then the opposite, pushing away into inaction or escaping from action.

The doer can arise in many ways and when it comes, it creates the illusion of you being separate from the action, you being separate from the existence.

Krishna describes the **formation of the I** through action and how impressions of I are created in form of the doer. What creates the doer? A desire can create the doer. If you do not take on your responsibility or duty, that can also form the doer. Escaping from necessary actions or procrastinating can form the doer. Attachment to the fruit of the action or attachment to the action itself will create the doer. All these fine things form the doer.

In the last chapter we saw that inaction will not make you reach liberation, neither will blind action. Krishna now details how, in the action you can stay in inaction, in a meditative spirit, in an **effortless action**. This state is what the sports people call being in the zone, in flow. When you are in love with something, playing music for example, you can play your instrument for hours and you do not even feel it. When a mother takes care of her child and is completely devoted to the mothering, her body may be tired, but her presence and being is in a very deep restful state. The same happens when a mountaineer is climbing a high mountain. His body is fully in action and the physical tiredness is there, but it is not tiring to his being or his presence. It is a soothing tiredness, which brings him a deep sleep in the night. This is effortless effort, or **inaction in action**, and this is what Krishna instructs Arjuna to aim for.

Now Krishna moves to another dimension saying, there is also **action in inaction**, which is samadhi. Krishna emphasises samadhi as the highest and greatest form of action. From outside, it may appear as nothing is happening, but samadhi is the greatest form of action. From outside there may be no action taking place, but the awareness of the jnana is there. That awareness, that seeing, that is-ness is the highest action.

This is Krishna's beautiful description of action and inaction, of living inaction in action and having the greatest action in inaction. It is a beautiful insight.

Often people ask, what does only seeing do? As maharishi Ramana is said, "see the seer". That is the highest form of action. Ramana, the great seer, a maharishi on a mountain in a state of absolute samadhi. What does presence of such a person do? It create ripples in the existence, in the streams of consciousness. Whenever and wherever there is an enlightened being, there are ripples of compassion and love created by the presence of such a being. And these ripples is the greatest action which is taking the humanity forward to flowering to evolution of consciousness as a whole.

This is the reason why, no matter from where people come, when they come to India they feel at home. This is the land which makes you feel at home. Why? It is the only country in the world that has recognised this form of action and taken care of these people. It is the only country that has been aware of these people. This country saw these people as the highest. That is because of Krishna, because of the great understanding of the Vedas, that it recognises the seer's work. It recognises the work of compassion. It recognises the work of action in total inaction, not inaction in inaction, as laziness or escaping from action. That is not what Krishna describes. In the previous chapter he clearly said, do your duty, and now he says, also know the highest form of action, samadhi, meditation. See meditation as an action and make it part of your life

After giving this insight, Krishna moves on to **yajña**. There is complete action and there is complete inaction, these are like two wings. Yajña is your way to reach to these two states. One is through the action, the other is through the presence, the seeing. Yajña is your way to reach to this.

As I explained in chapter three, one meaning of yajña is when you sit with the fire and put sacrifice and ghee into the fire and chant mantras. That yajña is usually understood as rituals and techniques of mantras, energy, prayers and visualization, but what is the underlying science of yajña, meant as the way of reaching the state of total action or total inaction.

Yajña in form of homa or fire ritual can be devoted to a particular deity, a manifestation of divine in a form. For example Lakshmi is a manifestation of abundance, of beauty, of life energy, abundance of life energy, health, wealth, and vitality. Visualise that, see it. And then giver prayers. For example, see the abundance entering your house, see the lack or the poverty leaving. Present the abundance with food, with happiness, with joy, and send the poverty outside the house. Visualize and create the yajña through visualization. Feel gratitude. In yajña you are giving, you are grateful. There is gratitude and visualization.

The yajña creates an energetic presence and takes away the negative aspects. It is done in a ritual setting, because rituals bring the metaphysical to the physical, to matter. Krishna describes yajña as the highest form of work.

There are other forms of yajña as well. For example, a dialogue can change into yajña if both people are dedicated to the truth. If they are not busy with their ego, wanting to win the debate, proving that their view is right or their understanding and their insight is superior to the other's, or establishing themselves as higher in the hierarchy of knowledge. No. When two people are dedicated to truth, and they enquire together for the sake of the truth, for the sake of reaching to clarity and insights, this conversation can change into yajña. When this conversation changes into yajña, when the dialogue, the work of thought, of reaching clarity and insights changes into yajña, it is beautiful. And yajña, Krishna says, is the highest form of work.

Yajña can also happen when you are doing your work. When you are dedicated to your work selflessly and you derive meaning and purpose from it, when it serves not only your own interest but a bigger interest of the community, of other people, of the family, of the future generation and you do it selflessly and full heartedly, your action changes into yajña.

Yajña can also happen in a relation, when love is at the centre, when the companionship or friendship is at the centre. When the possessiveness is not there and "my" and "mine" does not have any space. When ideas of how things should be is not there. When I, I, I, is not there. When the ego is not the focus, but love, devotion, relation and friendship is at the heart, the selfless giving is at the heart, then that relation, that friendship changes into yajña.

Here Krishna is reminding Arjuna to change his action into

yajña. He says, change your action in the battlefield, make it a yajña, make it the highest form, make it the path to nirvana. Krishna is guiding Arjuna beautifully, making a mundane action into something divine. Thousands of years ago this magnificent text was manifesting. In the midst of a chaotic battlefield, the greatest of the psychological, philosophical, religious and spiritual texts was taking birth. In that presence, in that friendship, Krishna is changing that very moment into divine through the power of yajña. And yajña is the highest, deepest and greatest form of work.

Krishna now moves the focus to understanding of **mastery**. What is mastery? For example, look at your attention. Is your attention under your mastery or is it being moved without you knowing it or wanting it? Today, all the social media companies are aiming for your attention. Big companies sell your attention to advertisers. the algorithms in apps in your phone are enslaving your focus. But are you mastering your attention? Are you free from being nudged into this and that, Are you able to think freely? Are you master of your thoughts? Are you master of your senses?

Krishna is telling Arjuna to **aim for mastery**. Aim for mastering your body through asanas. Aim for mastering your health through a good diet. Master your prana, your energy through pranayama. Master your mind through meditation, master your attention through awareness, master your awareness through consciousness and master your consciousness through love and devotion.

Krishna is giving a path of mastery to Arjuna, saying, be master of your own life. Do not let yourself be victim of circumstances and situations. Develop strength. Develop strength in your body through exercise and yoga, develop strength in your mind through meditation, develop strength in your attention through awareness and meditation and develop strength in your mind through practice, through seeing, through knowing what is, through knowing and understanding your mind and its manifestation in your life.

Develop **mastery of prana**. Krishna explains how a yogi is master of his or her prana. The yogi is aware of and is able to master the breath. Mastering the breath is central because the breath is always there. Whether it is the body, breath is there, whether it is attention, breath is there, whether it is awareness, breath is there, whether it is consciousness, breath is there. In all the phenomena breath is there, happening at the same time, and breath is directly connected to prana. So master pranayama and stay centred.

Focus the attention on the moment after inhalation and before exhalation, on the moment when the breath is taking the turn. At that moment what is taking place? Attention, pay attention to that.

Master the prana through the movement of the breath and through awareness of the breath as it. Also command your breath to be able to master it, because when you are able to do that, you are able to master your senses.

Master your senses. Krishna does not say escape or run away from the senses, he neither says blindly indulge in the senses. He says, master the senses. By mastering the senses, you can master the desire and develop master of the will. And when you master the desire and the will, you can be free.

What happens if you do not take care of your body? Sickness, illness and suffering would rule you. The same happens if you do not take care of the prana, lack of prana starts to rule you. Your thoughts are affected by your prana, so lack of prana would affect your thoughts. No matter what place you are in life the lack of prana will restrict you. You would be at the mercy of poverty of prana, similar to the lack of wealth. Mastery is the key. And with mastery, freedom starts to manifest.

After this, Krishna turns the attention to the **understanding of jnana** and the importance of seeing. Seeing as the great intertwinedness of karma yoga and jnana yoga, as Krishna says.

Here, I will point to Maharishi Ramana and Nisargadatta Maharaj, who are the finest and the greatest in making one understand what jnana is. These are the two giants who have clearly showed the path of jnana in the contemporary times. Maharishi Ramana says, ask "who am I?", ask this question. Do not just believe that you are Ātman. Ask this, who am I? Who am I? Who am I? Am I the body? Am I the mind? Am I the thought? Am I the attention? Am I the consciousness? Am I the heart? Am I the feelings? Am I the emotions? Am I the ego? Am I the self in form of karta and bhokta? The one who is experiencing life is bhokta. The one who takes, holds or gets attached to the action is karta. Or rogta, the complainer who plays the victim, poor me, poor me. Or am I drishta, the observer who is just watching all that? What is your true nature?

Swami Vivekananda goes a step further and says, "self-realisation is your duty". It is your greatest duty. Because if you do that duty, you do all the duties.

Krishna warns us not to escape our life for jnana, then jnana will not happen either. Because the path goes from here, not from anywhere else. The mind oversimplifies it and says, this is the way. Now I am going to leave everything and search for my true nature. No, it is not the way. The way still goes from wherever you are, whatever you are doing, in whatever situation you are. It does not go from somewhere out there in the Himalayas or in a retreat centre. You can go to all these places, but see it as a part of life, as everything else, not as the destination. Wherever you would go, you would take yourself along.

Jnana will create freedom in you, Krishna says. The greatest dimensions of freedom will manifest in your life. You will be free from everything, so live that freedom, as Krishna shows in his life. Krishna leads by example. He does not sit somewhere in a monastery or in some institution and claim to be the greatest guru. He is living it. He is a great musician. He is the finest political strategist. He is fighting along in the battlefield. He is the greatest philosopher and psychologist, the divine manifestation of an expression of love and compassion, This is what the freedom looks like.

And when you are going to live this freedom in your life, it will manifest in all dimensions. Because there is so much energy which goes to waste in the form of karta, bhokta, drishta, and rogta. You are not the poor me. And you are not that arrogant I who is doing everything. And neither are you that who is continuously seeking experiences and pleasures of life. Nor are you just a sheer observer. You are none of it. You are the eternal self, the Ātman, the Brahman, You are that. So know thyself, know thyself, know thyself. That is Krishna's message.

As Socrates expressed it, an unexamined life is not worth living. This is exactly what Krishna is saying, and way before. See your life through jnana, live your life through karma yoga. And do yajña. Make every aspect of your life into yajña. The path to nirvana, the path to consciousness is your divine right. Claim it, take it, receive it. Serve it.

In this chapter, Krishna also mentions the **different expressions of actions**. I would like to clarify this. He is describing different expressions of actions, not any form of caste or class system.

One expression of action is of thought, intellect, buddhi, seeing, attention, of consciousness and of knowledge. Another expression of action is of courage, of bravery, of prana, of responsibility, the action of advancement, moving forward in life, vision, and leading. Another type of action is of giving and receiving, management and decision making. Yet another expression of action is of serving, of doing, of physical actions, actions of consciousness which require repetition.

All these actions are inherent in all of us. There are some parts of these actions which start to develop and take shape in us and we naturally learn more of that action. From that typically our education takes place and we tend to get identified with that.

Jnana yoga says, do not get identified with the action. These are just sheer actions, no identification should take place in this.

In the modern times it is good to learn all of these actions. Bharat is the land of the Devas, who lead by the light and are lead by light, so do not let yourself be limited by the darkness of the ego into identification with one expression of action. Have the sharpest and brightest intellect. Have bravery, courage and ability to keep the values and standards to the highest. Be the best in trade and commerce, learn the best of the capital market, create and sell the best of the products to the world. And serve, and give, and have will to repeat the task, turn up day after day and deliver the best.

With time, effort and consciousness you would know your svadharma, an expression of action which gives you meaning and purpose and is natural and effortless to you. Nurture it and build deep roots in it. That will give you wings. No matter what, following your svadharma is far better than actions which are not natural expressions for you.

Chapter 5

The Pathless Path, the Dance of Divine

By now Arjuna has understood a lot about jnana, the understanding of inner knowledge, inner knowing, seeing as a seer. He has understood about Ātman and he has gained an understanding of action. But he is doubting. The idea of escaping is still there, that maybe going away from everything is the best path.

Krishna makes it clear that there is no distinction between the path of jnana and karma. **The paths are intertwined** and they are both happening at the same time. When you are in full action, it is the knowledge, the seeing, the awareness and the consciousness which brings the action to its full flowering. And when you enquire into your self asking "who am I", the jnana does not come to full flowering if you escape from action, if you escape from doing the right thing.

In our ancient history the rishis were following the way of jnana, living in the mountains and meditating. Yet many of the rishis had wives and children. They had schools and they were teachers. It is well documented how the rishis used to live in the forest and come back to the world to do their duty. After attaining the great state of consciousness or after learning the knowledge, they came back to teach. This is guru dakshina, the ancient Indian concept of repaying the guru after completing the education. It is giving thanks to the guru.

It is a big misunderstanding that the way is either or, either this or that. Krishna says that there is no distinction of the ways, they complement and support each other, only the centre differs. You can be on the path of jnana yoga, renouncing everything material and going away from the body, senses, thought and action. But you also have to do selfless action, either by serving the community as a teacher or taking care of the niti or shastra, the policy making. You can do this by understanding and commenting on different political aspects of life, as Chanakya, one of the greatest political thinkers. He was a sannyasin, yet acted as a royal advisor to the greatest empire. We have many examples like that, where the centre of learning is jnana yoga and renunciation is the way, but then there is total dedication to working for the community, for the country.

This is what Krishna says, that you cannot escape from action. If you are thinking of escaping from action by becoming a monk and then you have no action to be doing, that is a wrong way to go. Krishna says, when you are on the path of selfless action, then jnana is your greatest friend. Then know in every moment, in every action that you are not the doer. Do not get identified with your action, do not get identified with your thought, with your emotions, with the expression of your action. Be completely free from that and integrate the techniques of self-enquiry in your life.

Know thyself, know thyself. Aim for the salvation, aim for the liberation, aim for the enlightenment and awakening.

Krishna then describes how an enlightened being is master of his thoughts, emotions, senses and body. Aim for that mastery. For this mastery, the path of the jnana is the way forward.

The mind perceives the paths as separate, because the paths on the journey to a point in space and time are separate. But this is more like a quantum physics phenomenon where the photon is both a wave and a particle at the same time. The paths are not separate because it is a pathless land, as Jiddhu Krishnamurti said. It is a pathless land. There are no separate roads to reach Nirvana.

The idea that Nirvana is a destination that you will reach in the future is the biggest misconception which mind can have. Krishna clarifies this saying, you are not going anywhere. Nirvana is not somewhere out there. Salvation is here, this very moment. In this very body, this very mind, these very feelings, this very understanding. This is where the salvation is.

Krishna clarifies the matter of the paths further by saying, **the centre can be different**. The centre can be either of movement through selfless action or the centre can be of understanding or knowing through intellect, observing and seeing. In more recent times the mystic George Gurdjieff described three centres; the centre of heart, as devotion reaching the highest, the centre of intellect, as buddhi, knowing and seeing and the centre of movement, of action. 4000 years ago Krishna said the same, that you are not limited by any of these so-called paths, it is not either black or white. Later Adi Shankar and others who did commentaries on Bhagavad Gita called it karma sannyas yoga or sannyas karma yoga. Sannyas karma yoga was prescribed to the renounced monks and karma sannyas yoga was prescribed to the worldly householders.

But perceiving a sannyasin just by the clothes or just by the renunciation is not the right thing. There are many great sannyasins who do their daily job in government offices or in the shops or in the film industry, in art and culture. Krishna says, only a fool sees a sannyasin from the renunciation, and you are not that fool Arjuna. Do not renounce with the idea that you will get enlightenment by that. You are here in the battlefield, and this is what is available to you this moment, so follow your svadharma and bc truc to yoursclf.

Later, in Anugita Krishna prescribes periodical renunciation for Arjuna, saying, you can go away and come back again. But here in the battlefield he does not say that, he does not allow Arjuna to run away. This is not the moment for that. In Anugita, which comes after the battle is finished, when Krishna and Arjuna are lying under the banyan tree, there Krishna emphasises periodical renunciation.

I advice the same to people in modern times. It is good to take breaks away from your daily life so you can focus on self-enquiry. In the world it is easy to focus on meaning, purpose, passion and doing the right thing, doing your duty. It is easy to focus on following your passion, on finding your purpose and reaching to selfless service. It is easy to focus on mastering your senses and experiencing life. All these phenomena are easy in the world. But when it comes to self-enquiry it is good to have periodical renunciation, going away and turning the arrow of attention inwards.

Let us look at some **techniques for jnana**. One method is to see that "this very body is Brahman, this very thought is Brahman, this very being is Brahman". This technique and enquiring "who am I?" are two Vedantic techniques. One is exclusion, not this, not that and the other is inclusion, this body is Brahman, these senses are also Brahman, everything is Brahman. So see everything diligently, do not limit the seeing to body and mind like Charvaka, the ancient school who saw perception through senses and mind as the only source of knowledge. Go all the way, through the emotions, feelings, thought and thinking, to the seer, seeing and consciousness. All the way, paying attention, Samyaksamriti, the right attention, the right remembrance as Buddha said.

So periodical renunciation only comes later for Arjuna, after the battle has been won. Then Arjuna is told by Krishna that now it is time to pay attention to the self-enquiry. Self-enquiry is at the heart of karma yoga and karma yoga is at the heart of self-enquiry. A renunciate who is doing his duties for the community or society is as important as a householder on the inner path with the responsibility of family. Krishna prescribes meditation techniques for both.

If you do not understand **Karma Yoga**, if finding meaning and purpose seems too complex, then Krishna simplifies it. He gives a simple insight to Arjuna. Simply **devote your action to the divine**, devote your action to Ishvara. Not the usual understanding as someone somewhere out there, but the divine presence, the divine manifestation of Ishvara in life as whole, as this very existence. Devote your action to that and devote your life in the service of the divine. Krishna is simplifying karma yoga for Arjuna, saying that it is about devotion, that your action is in devotion, that you are not busy with I, "I am the one doing". How the action can lead to ego is through I, me, my, us, they, them. Also the ego of the God, of my God. Do not limit your action by putting it into these small frames of I, me and my. Free the action from this. Let your action be in service of the divine. This is a vast sphere, an infinite sphere.

If you see, in the modern day context, there are people motivated by finite and people motivated by infinite, and in longer run the people motivated by infinite always win. Take the example of the Wright brothers who wanted to take the humanity forward by creating a flying machine. There were many others at the same time working on creating the first flying machine, but the others were motivated by salaries and other limited goals like ego and status. But the purpose of the Wright Brothers was so clear, wanting to fly, wanting to take humanity forward. They were in the bigger sphere. Their motivation was not finite, it was an infinite purpose of freedom, of not being limited by gravitation but actually flying, of adventure and exploration.

Now Krishna is going a step further, saying, do not limit your actions to that either, but give your action to divine, to the infinite. Then your actions suddenly become vast and infinite and you have infinite energy available to you and you are no longer limited.

Take exercise as an example. Many people do exercise in order to achieve better flexibility, gain muscular strength or loose weight, and that is fine. But when you take care of your body as a temple of the divine, as an artist gently sculpts a statue, then you see the health and get in touch with the vitality of the body whereby you take better care of it. The goal has changed from finite to infinite as care, health and vitality are infinite.

Krishna then takes it even a step further, to the divine, because for beauty and vitality you still need the senses and the body. Living is limited to senses and body, but the divine is not limited to senses and body, it is not limited to emotions and thought. So devote your action to the divine.

Krishna is masterfully changing Arjuna's perspective. If Arjuna is finding karma yoga complex, as in the previous chapter, Krishna simplifies it for him. Understand that the previous chapter dealt with very complex phenomena. It is not easy to understand the Karma Yoga, it is complex, but here Krishna says, if it is difficult then simply devote your action to the divine. Do not get attached to the action or its results, do not create the I and do not limit your actions with simplistic attachments. Have the luxury of living a life of flow, of beauty and serenity.

Then Krishna says that, as a self-liberated being you see the **interconnectedness of life**. You see how everything is interconnected, how everything matters and is equally important. You cannot live without water or without sun. If one day the sun does not rise, the whole humanity is over. Everything is equally important and interconnected. This is the case with the body also, Krishna says. You cannot say that the body is lower or that intellect is superior. Everything has its importance and everything is interconnected.

Rather than seeing things separately, see things as harmonious and interconnected, as one ecosystem. See the body as an ecosystem and do not try to correct things separately. If the prana in the body increases, the whole body gets healthier, and if the body gets healthy, prana will increase and your thoughts will be clearer. So see the ecosystem in everything. This, Krishna says, is how a liberated being sees the world. He sees an elephant, a monk, a cow and a plant as the same. Krishna points out to see the whole ecosystem in everything.

That principle can be applied today as well. In the economy, you cannot say that this company is higher or that some individual's shop is lower. You cannot say that because it is all an interconnected system. You cannot put one at the centre and others at the periphery. It is the same in the nature. Everything matters and there is an inner dynamic that flows by itself, and that is perfectly fine. There is an internal dynamic in this.

With this understanding there comes a sense of **equanimity**, a sense of clarity to see the interconnectedness in one's being.

A liberated being sees the world like this, and by seeing the world like this, that person leads by example. This is the essential understanding of the interconnectedness.

Krishna mentions the importance of developing a **consciousness of and respect for life in general**, whether your centre is with self-enquiry, with the karma yoga or however you live. Develop a deep respect for life. A life affirmative attitude is a crucial principle on which you can base the journey to Nirvana, to liberation. Because if you do not have that life affirmative attitude, sooner or later you are bound to get corrupted by power or by something else the purity of heart would disappear. And the purity of heart, mastery of the senses, mastery of the body and prana, this lies at the root of the inner path. Taking care of this is central, Krishna says. Do not let your heart and thoughts become corrupted. Keep the purity and gentleness, the tenderness of the heart. It is very important. The way to protect this is by being life affirmative, by respecting life in general.

Now Krishna goes on to the next subject, understanding how to **master the body and the senses**. Krishna does not instruct to suppress and close down your senses, as if they do not exist, like an ostrich. He neither says to blindly indulge in pleasure seeking. He says master the body and senses.

To master the senses, he says, one must **master one's emotions**. To master emotions first understand them. Know what fear is and do not let it move you. Know how it originates, what kind of thoughts trigger it. See the physiology of fear, what happens in the body when the instinct of fight, flight, freeze or please is triggered. Understand greed, how you get moved and nudged by companies to buy products and services. See your greed for success and how quickly you discourage yourself when the failure hits you. Understand anger and how it originates. What makes you angry? Is your anger associated with ego? Is it your ego wanting to dominate and control the changing circumstances? Understand anger and do not be scared of it.

These are natural instincts in humans. There is a fight-flight-freeze instinct in you which is coupled with the emotion of fear. There is an instinct of sexuality, there is an instinct of anger. These are natural phenomena in humans, so do not be scared of them. Neither fall blindly prey to them nor ignorantly escape and run away from them. Understand the instincts, master them through understanding, master them through bravery and courage, master them through practice.

Mastering emotions and instincts like this, Krishna says, is the way to master senses, master thoughts, master the mind, master the body and master the pranayama. This is the secret Krishna is giving here. Mastering your emotions will make you master of your decisions, and when you master both your decisions, senses, body and prana, then you are master of your life. Nobody before spoke so beautifully about mastery as Krishna does here.

In modern times this translates to having a **growth mindset** instead of a fixed mindset, not getting disappointed by failure, not focusing so much on winning that you forget everything else. So drop the fixed mindset and develop a mindset of growth instead. Anything can be learned. See failure as a stepping stone and rise up again when you fall. See winning as nothing more than a small celebration on the way. See life in this way. With a growth mindset your life will flower towards mastery of your life. You will not be a victim, but a master of your own life.

While gaining this mastery, know that the mastery is not for the ego. **Dedicate your mastery to the divine**. Master yourself for the service of the divine. Sometime what happens, you master something and with the mastery the ego comes, and then ego masters you. When winning in life you will get successful, and with the success the ego comes, but then the ego fails you.

The Armenian mystic George Gurjieff said that you have no soul unless you work for it. Krishna goes a step further than that. He says, Ātman is your greatest friend but also your greatest enemy. How can Ātman be your enemy? When you do not master your life, when you do not dedicate your life to the divine, then Ātman becomes enemy, because the cycle of birth and rebirth is a prison and now you are not escaping it, and Ātman is an infinite source of energy available to you. Imagine if you are bound by something and there is infinite energy available to you, then that infinite energy becomes your enemy. But infinite energy means infinite life is available to you, so you would be stuck repeating the same, over and over again. This is how Ātman becomes your enemy. But Ātman becomes your friend when you free yourself by mastering your life, by dedicating and devoting your actions and your mastery to the divine, by knowing yourself, by understanding and seeing. Then Ātman becomes your greatest friend. And eventually you will see yourself as Ātman and liberation is bestowed upon you. You are the blessed one, and that is your true self, the blessed one.

So go for it. Do not feel limited by your circumstances. Self-enquiry is the way to mastery and mastery is the way to self-enquiry. Krishna instructs to master yourself and then do the self-enquiry. Action and self-enquiry, action, self-enquiry. It is like walking, one step with one foot and then one step with the other.

Earlier Krishna said that the path goes through action, through mastery of emotions, through growth mindset, and now he is going further, saying that you can only truly gain mastery when you know yourself, when you know that you are not your emotions, when you know that you are not your feelings, when you know that this is also divine, it is not separate. Your life in itself is divine, the whole life is divine. Knowing yourself through self-enquiry, Krishna says, is the only way with which you can truly free yourself. It is the way to truly winning.

For **mastering prana**, understand it through different techniques of **pranayama**. Master your breath in different situations, with different emotions. Master the senses through the breath. If you master your breath, you can master your senses and if you master your senses you can master your body. In the previous chapter a meditation technique was introduced, a type of pranayama where one is aware of the gap between the inhalation and exhalation. Krishna has also introduced another technique, watching the breath the way it is without changing it. There are many other pranayamas, for example pranayamas to keep your breath healthy, like bhastrika pranayama, a quick and intensive breathing and kapalbhati pranayama which is cleansing through intensive exhalations. Understand the science of pranayama and integrate pranayama techniques in your daily life.

Master your breath while being in action. See how your breath changes when you indulge in food. See how it changes when you have angry thoughts and how it changes with sexuality.

Be aware of the breath and be aware of the sensations in the breath. This is the pranayama from earlier, where Krishna gave a short shloka on it. When the shloka is elaborated, it leads you to understanding pranayama and integrating the energy of the prana, to mastery of prana in the daily life, to watching prana and the breath, watching the way it is, to seeing the connection of prana with thought, seeing the connection of prana with emotions, seeing the connection of prana with the body.

Krishna now gives a **meditation technique for seeing the seer**. He says, pay attention to the place in between your eyes, with eyes half closed, half open. There is a place in between your eyes, at the centre of your skull. Bring your attention here and see the seer. Know the knower. This is the technique Krishna describes. It is one of the oldest techniques.

In the Buddhist tradition the technique of vipassana or watching the way it is has been really elaborated with understanding the relation of the prana to thoughts and to emotions, seeing the sensations in the body with the breath, seeing the movement of the breath. They have worked in depth with this. The yogic and tantric traditions have worked on prana through mastering the breath, understanding the movement of the prana and how to directly master prana through interconnectedness. These two traditions have worked on that.

Vedanta has worked on the meditation technique for seeing the seer that Krishna describes here. Everything in Vedanta indirectly comes down to this, what is called direct experience. The technique that Krishna gives here is a simpler version of the Vedantic techniques from Upanishads for seeing the seer, knowing oneself, vid vidya, ved vedanta. This is the Vedanta. With your consciousness flowering you see the seer itself, you know the knower itself and there is no difference between jnana and jnani. There is no difference between knowledge, knower and knowingness. It all becomes one. This is a foundational technique, and it is important to remember that this technique is the way to liberation, to transformation, to knowing yourself.

Integrate these techniques in your life. If you give a certain time to these techniques, your life would become very different.

Chapter 6

Deep Within the Stillness, the Truth Begins to Sing

Chapter six is one of the most beautiful chapters of Bhagavad Gita. It was also the **favourite chapter of Swami Vivekananda.** He loved this chapter and suggested reading it to every young person in adolescence, in the twenties or who is just moving in the world. This was the counsel of Swami Vivekananda, that this is the chapter for you. And in my understanding, this is the chapter that Buddha was inspired by. When you really understand and know this chapter, there is nothing that can stop you from self-realization. That is how important this chapter is. This is where Krishna tells exactly what you need. He describes everything with such clarity and simplicity, that when read it, you feel awe. What an understanding, what an insight, and what an expression. If it is not possible for you to read the whole Bhagavad Gita, just read this chapter, that is enough, because everything you need on the path to self-realisation is covered here.

When the chapter begins, we start with Arjuna. Arjuna being who he is, a simple seeker, he asks, still tell me, is the path of selfless action superior or is the path of self-enquiry, of jnana superior? Krishna has already explained this, but one more time he says that it is foolish to distinct between these ways, because they are intertwined, they are interconnected. On the path of selfless action, where you devote your action to the divine, where your motivations are not finite but infinite, where you serve through action, on that path self-enquiry plays a key role. And on the **path of self-enquiry,** where you directly inquire into the nature of Ātman and Brahman and into the nature of reality, you cannot be away from action. Action is a part of that expression as well.

But Arjuna is insisting, so Krishna says, it is easier to go into inner inquiry if you just drop action and continuously follow the self-enquiry, but if you dedicated your life to self-enquiry and dropped all action, that would not be the right path. Do not drop action, do not drop your duties. If you choose to walk on the path of the sannyasin, if you decide that you want to dedicate your life for self-realisation, then do not drop action. Stay committed to action. This is Krishna's clarity on this.

Krishna again explains that when you are on the path of selfless action and self-enquiry, Ātman becomes your friend, supporting you on the path, the **divine becomes your friend and supports you on the path**. With Arjuna the divine literally manifested in the form of Krishna, a friend, master and guru. That tells something about Arjuna's seeking and about the depth of his longing. It also shows how the divine literally comes in your life as a friend and as a guide. Life becomes a guide. Your inner Ātman, your inner guru becomes your guide.

But if you are on the path of life without this inner

understanding, just living for and by limited ideas and ideologies, limited structures of time and space, then you can keep on going in that direction, as there is infinite energy of Ātman available to you. In this way you become your own enemy. Ātman is neutral, but you become your own enemy. It is like riding carelessly at a high speed in a car with infinite gas. Ātman is that infinite source of energy which keeps bringing you to birth and rebirth, again and again. And you are trapped in your own misery. There is no way out from that misery. You are doomed to stay in that misery, because Ātman is not letting you go. It is an infinite source of energy, and now you are bringing that infinite source of energy to misery.

When people hit the jackpot in lottery, their life rarely gets better. Often it gets worse as their misery is enhanced with extra resources. It is similar with the divine, Ātman, it is the infinite source of energy available to you. It is your freedom, Ātman will not come in your way. It is your freedom to choose, and the moment you choose the path of karam sannyas yoga or sannyas karam yoga, the divine comes as a friend, as a guide, as a master and a guru to you.

This is a splendid portrayal Krishna gives of becoming one's own enemy when living a life without devotion, without dedication to passion, meaning and purpose, to selflessly serving something greater than your limited self. It shows how the manifestation of truth and beauty does not happen if you do not enquire, if you do not examine your life. I love when Socrates says, "an unexamined life is not worth living". This is a beautiful statement, and that is exactly what Krishna says. Examine your life. Live a life of self-enquiry and dedicate your action in the service of the divine. This brings equanimity in your life.

When you walk on this path, Krishna says, you become a

true yogi and **equanimity** comes in your life. Then you can go through the greatest challenges unmoved. The misery can no longer touch you. Nothing reaches you. Your inner state stays peaceful and in equanimity in the most difficult times as well as in the greatest and brightest times.

This is what he is saying, that when the true yoga starts to flower in you, this is how it manifests in your life, this is how your life flowers in many different dimensions.

It is like an ocean. You literally become one with the ocean. Ocean is ocean, it is not identified with the waves. Even when there is storm and thunder on the surface and the waves are huge, it does not reach the deepest part of the ocean. That is what Krishna describes, that state of equanimity and peace at the deepest core. The equanimity is there, even in the wildest and most turbulent times. If you are identified with the surface only and not exploring the depth of your consciousness, then when the storm comes, most likely your boat will break or you will break. But if you go to the depth of the ocean, and you see ocean as you and you as ocean and there is no separation between the two, then the waves are just a part of life. The waves are like the world. It is all the all the senses, all the actions of the world, all your desires, ambitions. All that is happening on the surface, but at the deepest place there is equanimity and peacefulness.

Krishna says, from this peacefulness a **deep compassion** comes, and you start to see everything as equally important, every aspect as equally important, every time of the day as equally important, and every dimension of life as equally important. You do not see things as higher or lower. Everything becomes important.

Understanding that, Krishna says, you will see that this battle is as important as your self-enquiry, or self-enquiry is as important as your selfless action of service. So take your bow and stand with your bow upright and face the difficult situation in front of you. Do not shy away from it, do not escape from it, do not run away from it. That is the beautiful insight Krishna is giving to Arjuna.

Then Krishna goes on to describe **the state of consciousness of the liberated one**. In that state there is infinite compassion and infinite equanimity. It is like the ocean, where the peacefulness and equanimity is at the depths of the ocean, and infinite compassion is manifesting through the equanimity into the life. The allegory of ocean is wonderful, because the ocean is vast and full of life, and that is the compassion of the ocean. So many beings are living in that ocean, and there is equanimity at the heart of the ocean, even when the greatest of the waves and tsunamis come. So ocean is a wonderful allegory of the liberated being.

Krishna says, aim for this, because this is who you are. Go for it, do not hesitate. It is your divine right, it is your birth right, so aim for it. And when you aim for it, when you start going in the direction of the divine, then Ātman comes as your friend and guides you. In Arjun's case it is happening in a literal sense. The divine is his friend, the divine is his master, his guide, his guru. This shows Arjun's sincerity.

Now Arjuna asks a question with the utmost sincerity. He says, oh great Krishna, I completely understand you, but my mind is like the wind. It is a flickering mind. What you say is great, but please try to understand the state of my mind.

Krishna smiles and says, yes, this is **the nature of mind**. Mind is flickering. Mind is like the wind. Do not expect anything else from it. It is the surface of the vast ocean. Mind is a new manifestation in this vast ocean, but is the surface only. The greater the size of the ocean, the greater will be the movements or the waves on the surface. This is how the nature of the mind is. But it can be mastered.

Krishna now describes **the middle path**, which is about creating a harmony in your life. It is not about sleeping too much or sleeping too little, it is not about eating too much not too little, it is not about indulging completely in pleasures or completely shying away from it. It is about living a healthy, good life. That is the beginning. That is the balance. What Krishna says is to find a good balance in life and reflect that balance into your practice.

Then he gives Arjuna one of the most ancient techniques, which many yogis in the past were practicing. It is **a technique of the middle path**, which everyone should learn and understand, and this is why Swami Vivekananda insisted so much that one should read this chapter. Krishna says, find a space which is neither too high, nor too low, and away from everything. Go into your aloneness and sit with your back straight. Neither too high, nor too low, up from the ground and well insulated. In the past you put deer skin or dried grass on the ground for this. Find a well insulated space, neither too high nor too low, neither too discomfortable nor too comfortable. In that space sit with your back straight, head high, hands resting on your knees or onto your feet in the Buddha posture. In this pose this let your mind calm down. When your eyes are neither open nor closed, your gaze naturally comes towards the tip of the nose, so keep your eyes half open. Be aware. Be watchful of everything, all your senses, all your emotions, feelings, sensations in the body, your thoughts or the thinking. Be aware and watchful of every aspect of the present moment. See it, be watchful of it, be aware of it. Be aware of yourself, be aware of the seer, be aware of the one who is aware. Pay attention to the very consciousness, pay attention to to the very attention itself.

Pay attention to the awareness itself and be aware in this state.

Krishna clearly instructs to **practice this technique with vigour**. If you have not eaten or not taken care of your health, there will not be much vigour. There must be vitality in the body, vigour in the energy. Your body and your being must be full of prana from a day of good action, a good night's sleep and a good diet. With body and prana full of vigour and vitality practice the technique. Practice it with determination and discipline. Practice it with full dedication, utmost dedication, knowing that this is the moment, this is the door to divine.

Dedicate this practice to the divine, to Krishna himself, to divine consciousness. When you dedicate the meditation for the greater good, that inaction becomes the greatest action. By devoting this technique to the divine, you are doing the greatest action in this inaction.

In this way you will find the core, the heart of the ocean, and you will know compassion. This compassion will reach to all living beings, to every aspect of life. The ripples of this compassion will reach to all dimensions of life and every aspect of living.

In the Zen tradition they call this technique Zazen, just sitting doing nothing. This is what Krishna says. Sit, just sit. Be aware of everything, neither particularly aware of breathing nor particularly aware of anything else. It is a middle path. Your eyes are neither open nor closed, you are neither high up nor low on the floor. Your prana is full of vigour, your body is full of vitality, and there is determination, dedication and devoting the practice to the divine, to the greater.

Do not make this technique about reaching somewhere, becoming goal oriented. Devote this technique to the divine as a gift, as an offering to divine. As an offering you are doing it, for compassion, for the greater good, for the divine, in servitude to the divine.

When you do this servitude, divine comes as your guide, as your help, as your brother, as your sister, guiding you in your daily life. Trust that. In this way the technique becomes your prayer. Make it your action, your dharma, and make your practice a prayer by dedicating it to the divine.

Take good care of yourself by having a **balanced life**. Let this practice be done on the foundation of a balanced life. On the foundation of balanced life practice this technique, as a dedicated technique on the path of the divine, offering it as a prayer. This inaction becomes the highest form of action in the service of the divine. Krishna shows beautifully how this technique can become your path to divine.

With this understanding Krishna has given almost everything. He has shown us **the royal path**, as Swami Vivekananda called it. See, by this time Krishna has given clarity on finding your dharma and dedicating yourself to it through the path of action, meaning, purpose, practice and passion and devoting this action to the infinite. He also showed the path of self-inquiry, knowing oneself, examining and seeing, continuing the negation until you reach to the very essence of Ātman. And now he has showed us the daily meditation practice of the yogi and instructed us to devote this technique to the divine, laying the foundation of prayer and devotion. The combination of these three ways is the royal path.

In the next chapter Krishna will go much deeper into the path of the devotion, because when there is devotion, every path becomes a joyful celebration. Without devotion you are dependent on determination and discipline. Devotion adds another flavour as the divine is there in your life, present as your beloved, as your sakha or friend, as your guru. That is the next chapter.

But Arjuna is not stopping here. He says, my dear brother, oh great Krishna, oh divine Krishna, I understand what you are saying, but I know myself also. What if I fall from from the path as you described? What if I am not so determined, if I am not such a great devotee, if I am not able to self-inquire, what then?

Krishna answers him saying, my dear friend, do not be worried about that. Yes, be aware that this is the path. This is walking on a razor's edge, it is a royal path, and it does require great responsibility, great diligence, great awareness, and great sincerity. It is the path of the prince, the royal. With this path, I have given you all different dimensions. But let us say that you have fallen from the path. Do not let that thought stop you walking on the path, because the good deeds you acquire from it saves you, brings you good karma, and your life will transform.

In modern times, especially in the West, a single aspect of yoga, the asanas, is being taught, without the full context of yoga. From the standard of Krishna, practising this diluted yoga is equal to having fallen from the path. But still, great health is born from it. Propagating asanas is a good deed, as it brings good health and a long life to whomsoever practices it. There are also people who have reduced this royal path to a certain form of dogmatic activity. Even those people who have fallen from the path are living a life of joy and celebration. That is what Krishna is saying. So do not let this thought stop you from walking the path. Even in its fallen state it is a great path, it is a path of royalty. This is what Krishna is saying.

Krishna then explains that there are **different levels of prayer**. You can pray and ask for material good. You can pray and ask for good health. You can dedicate your life to the divine without asking anything, and that will be a prayer. You can practice self-enquiry, karma yoga and meditation and through that know yourself and then go and pray in the form of gratitude, saying, oh great Krishna, oh great divine, thank you so much, my life is such a blessing. That is the highest form of prayer, Krishna says. So do not let yourself be limited by the thought that you are going and asking for something material. That is fine, go and ask for it.

Let this yajña of life flower in your life. Start from anywhere. Start.

Krishna now says to Arjuna, oh great warrior, give your dedication, your determination, vigour and vitality to this divine path. Serve the infinity, the divine infinite in you. And the divine infinite will bestow upon you friendship, guidance, love and compassion. This is bound to happen. So trust, and welcome to the path of royals, where there is divine prayer, where there is selfless action and deep self-enquiry. Integrate this in your life. Let it be your life.

Chapter 7

The Secret is Hidden Where the Mortal Feet Can't Reach

I call chapter seven the song of the divine. It is about **knowing the mystical force** which people from all over the world at different times have tried to describe. Some call it God, some call it the power beyond, some call it manifestation of that which cannot be understood, which cannot be put into any idea or any imagination.

This mystical force is always there. We all feel it and sense it, yet we cannot point specifically to it, and the scientists are unable to figure out how this universe exists and why it exists. There is no answer to that. We have discovered what gravitation does and how it works, but we do not know why. We have discovered how the universe was created, but we do not know why. The creation of this universe, the divine principle, the fundamental principle of life which is in life and beyond. Call it by any name. Call it Ishvara, call it God, call it by any other name. It is that with which the very source of life takes birth, the very universe takes birth. Knowing this, seeing this, is liberation in itself.

In this chapter Krishna says to Arjuna, oh Parth, oh my dear friend. You have taken refuge in me, the divine consciousness, Ishvara consciousness, practicing yoga with devotion.

In the previous chapter Krishna started giving the key of the devotion by explaining that all the yogas, self-enquiry, selfless action, awareness and meditation, all the yoga have devotion as the core. Now Krishna starts giving **guidance on devotion**. He says, practicing yoga with devotion you shall know me beyond any doubt as all perfection, as all perfect Ātman in all beings.

What he means by this is, that through devotion, you will know me. Not me as the person standing in front of Arjuna, because of course Arjuna knows that it is Krishna, who is my brother and my friend, but know me in my original self. This body and this birth is happening far away from Krishna, but for Arjuna it is the reality. At that moment, Arjuna is holding the feet of Krishna, and those feet are the reality. But here, Krishna is inviting Arjuna to know him beyond the form.

Krishna says, I shall fully teach you this knowledge as well as all pervasive actions that results from realisation of divine, of God after which there remains nothing better in this world to know.

What he means is, that this alchemy, this key to all yoga which he is introducing now, after this there is nothing left to be known. This is **the call of devotion**. Krishna says, know that this is your birthright, that this is the purpose for which you were born.

He says, hardly does one among thousands strive to know me, and hardly does one among the thousands who strive for this know my essence.

Among hundreds of thousands of people, only a few choose to walk the inner path, and out of those few, even fewer get the essence, the devotion in their heart. So, if even for a moment you have known the peacefulness or silence of meditation, if even for a moment you have tasted the nectar of devotion, if even for a moment you have known the flow of selfless action, then you know the diamond which cannot be bought by neither power nor money. Then you have that. You have gone beyond any great success in this world because you have tasted this. Neither the great conqueror Alexander nor the mighty Genghis Khan could reach there, even if they had conquered the whole world. The wealthiest cannot buy it. This diamond is a gift, and it is a gift that only the divine bestows.

If you have received this gift, then you are the chosen one, you are the one. If you have this diamond, then know yourself as the chosen one, that is what Krishna says. Then do not see yourself as everybody else, because by sheer experience of this devotion, by sheer experience of this silence, by sheer experience of this peacefulness in your heart, even if only for a moment, you are chosen to walk on the path to divine, to know the divine, to know. Your invitation has been sent from the infinity, which means that you are chosen so come along on this path.

See this. See the importance of it. Do not let this be lost in the chaos of the world. This is a pearl, and as the Bible says, one should not throw pearls for swine. Cherish those diamonds, those pearls that have been given to you. Do not throw them to the swine of worldly chaos and disorder, which is repetitive and ignorant. Know your value. Know that you are chosen. See yourself as that. Accept the invitation and come to the divine.

Hardly does one among the thousands strive to know me,

hardly does one among the thousands who strive for this know my essence, Krishna says.

He adds, I am the creator of all nature with all it's dimensions. Water, fire, wind, sky, mind, buddhi, and the sense of self.

All the space and time comes from this **divine principle**. Trying to name this would be an illusion, but for the sake of communication, we could call this indescribable divine principle Ishvara consciousness. From this Ishvara consciousness all the dimensions are born. All the dimensions of space and time as well as all the elements in it has taken birth from this. From all the elements, the essence of a drop in form of the individual self has taken birth.

Let us look at it again. Ishvara consciousness manifests in space and time. Space and time manifest in the collective cosmic consciousness. And from the collective cosmic consciousness, as a drop, the individual soul or spirit takes place. And in the individual spirit and soul, the sense of I manifests. In that sense of self, the perception of awareness, attention takes place. From the awareness and attention, buddhi comes. From the collective mind, the individual mind in form of manas manifests, and from the manas all the senses find their roots, and from the senses the body takes birth. This is how you come into existence.

This is a beautiful process of **manifestation of the divine principle**, in the end giving birth to you as an individual. So you are not separate from the divine. The divine is at the root of your existence. Therefore do not see yourself as separate from the divine. You are the essence of the divine.

Know the divine through devotion, through yoga, through knowing. Walk on the path of the divine, and the divine will come to guide you, to support you in the form of a friend, a brother or a divine guide, like Krishna himself.

Krishna now says, this nature, oh mighty armed is the lower insensate nature. But against it there is my consciousness, the living nature which animates the whole world.

Krishna is here reminding Arjuna that his presence, this physical presence that you see and know, is a manifestation of the divine. But beyond that, there is a vast and deep ocean full of life. This ocean is infinitely vast with infinite consciousness. And when you look up in the sky, you see billions of galaxies. Each and every galaxy has billions of stars, and each star has planets, and those planets may have life. So imagine how much life this existence has.

See the divine principle which has given birth to so much life. Know that divine principle. Do not be stuck in the illusion of the physical form of Krishna, because that physical form is just a mere reflection or manifestation of this vastness, of this infinite consciousness.

This is accessible to you through Ātman. So walk on the path of Ātman. Make the path to Ātman a divine celebration through devotion. Be in devotion to the divine, be in devotion to Krishna, be in devotion to the divine principle in you, beyond you, from you, through you and the one which has given birth to you in all the universe. Do not see it as limited to you. The infinite principle is all and everywhere. Know that.

Know that all beings arise from this true nature, and that I am both the creator and the end of the world, Krishna says.

This is a beautiful one, **Purusha and Prakṛti**. This is where Sāṃkhya describes the consciousness and the matter or nature. Everything in this whole existence comes from these two divine principles. If there were no consciousness in this universe, there would be no life, and if there were no matter, there would be no life either. All the life we know, in all its mutations and evolution as Darwin expresses it, all this life comes from the meeting of these two divine principles, Prakṛti or nature and Purusha or divine consciousness. In the melting pot of divine consciousness and nature, that is where life is born. So wherever you see life, you will find consciousness meeting the mother nature.

This is how evolution happens. Life is constantly evolving, and with that consciousness is constantly evolving. Consciousness in the form of life is evolving. Absolute consciousness was, is, and always would be absolute. For the absolute consciousness, this divine manifestation of life, in form of human beings, in form of you, this is the very expression of devotion. Life is expression of the heart of divine. So, when you are in devotion, you are divine, you are an expression of the divine, you are the very medium of the divine. Know yourself as that.

This is a beautiful expression of being in love with the divine, knowing the divine, not limiting yourself as separate, but seeing yourself as originating from divine and then melting and dissolving in the divine.

"All know that the drop merges into the ocean, but few know that the ocean merges into the drop", the mystic poet Kabir said. Did the drop merge with the ocean or the ocean with the drop? See that the ocean is waiting to be merging into this drop, and this drop is born to merge back into the ocean.

Now Krishna clarifies for Arjuna, that he should **see this world as Maya**. Maya means illusion. He adds, but know that this illusion is also me. Do not see the illusion as separate from me. Everything you can imagine is me. So, it is perfectly fine to be in love and create an imagination of me in human form, as in the form of Krishna and Radha, and to be in love with this form and get inspired by it. But do not be limited to that. The true me is hiding behind the Maya, or Yogamaya as Krishna says. So be brave enough to reach to my heart, to marry my core. I am inviting you through my human form, inspiring you through my life story, through Bhagavad Gita, so come. Get inspired by and be in love with my human form. See my human form as a manifestation, but know that I am hiding behind the Yogamaya. Transcendent the Yogamāyā and reach to me.

Krishna also instructs Arjuna to pray. **Pray to your ishta-deva.** Pray to your ishta, for example the manifestation of abundance in form of ma Lakshmi. Your ishta will bring you the very essence and life nectar, but in the end what we seek is the divine consciousness or Ishvara consciousness. Melt into that divine consciousness. Pray to your ishta and seek guidance. Seek courage and valour from the great Hanuman, seek abundance from mother Mahalakshmi, and seek wisdom from sri Ganesha and ma Saraswati.

It is the divine consciousness from which the transformation will come, where you will meet the very source of life. So aim for the very source of life. **Know the divine principle**, the absolute principle. It is important to understand that it is the manifestion of Ishvara principle itself–in form of bhakti for ishtadeva, or longing to meet the divine, or rising vairagya in one's heart for the world or bhakti rasa in devotion, as the divine love of Radha and Krishna. So, know the divine principle through devotion in all its dimensions. Through love, through surrender, through bhaktirasa. All this is part of the journey. Live that journey as a whole.

Now Krishna moves on to describe **four kinds of devotees**. The first is a devotee for material gains, the second is when one is in distress, one is in devotion, and the third is devotee just for being in love with the divine. The fourth kind of devotee is when one is totally dedicated to bhakti, to self-enquiry, to selfless action and to meditation and thereby bound to liberation, yet one is fully surrendered in devotion. This is the highest form of devotion, Krishna says. Aim for being such a devotee.

It is perfectly fine to ask the divine for material gains and success and also to call for the divine as a help in distress. Both are perfectly fine. But the next stage of devotion is being in love with the divine just for sake of being in love, knowing the divine for the sake of knowing the divine. And then the higher stage of devotion, the devotion of a liberated being, one who has known himself through self-enquiry, whose action is pure through selfless service, who has known inner peace and awakening through meditation and yet is a devotee.

This is the beautiful **nature of the bhakta**. Surrender is the power of bhakta.

Krishna and Arjuna have a flag of Hanuman on their rath, and Hanuman is such a liberated being in devotion. Hanuman is sitting and watching over everything from above. In the ancient stories, it is sometimes mentioned that Hanuman is sitting and listening to Bhagavad Gita from the rath. These stories are poetic expressions highlighting that one more person is present and listening, and this is exactly such a devotee as Krishna describes, a liberated being who is fully in devotion to the form of Vishnu previously manifested as Rama and now as Krishna. He is there with them, all the way through the battle.

The greatest form of devotion is this, when one knows oneself, when one's action is pure, when there is awakening in one's life, yet one is fully dedicated and devoted to the divine principle. Aim for that. Do not aim for enlightenment only for the sake of enlightenment. You can achieve siddhis or great powers and awakening through meditation, but then that awakening and siddhi is not complete, because the illusion of the ego and the self would remain.

Purify your action through compassion and selfless service when you enter into self-enquiry. Know yourself to the purest, that you are Ātman and Brahman, nothing less than that. Know that. Devote all the compassion of selfless action, all the knowledge, the jnana which comes from self-enquiry, and all the awakening of the consciousness which comes from meditation, devote it all to the divine. Now there is nothing left and only divine. You are a divine manifestation through this.

This is **complete enlightenment** that Krishna is describing. Aim for that. And when you aim for that, you would be the ocean itself and the drop. Taste the ocean, it is the same wherever you are, and the same would be your nature. You would be the divine in every essence and every form, and there would be no distinction between matter and consciousness, no distinction between mundane and divine. Everything would become divine for you because you would be a divine manifestation in devotion. This is the power of the devotion that Krishna is describing here.

Next Krishna depicts how **Maya manifests in form of the three gunas**, sattva, rajas and tamas. Krishna says that these gunas are all Maya, but they are important for you to know and understand. Yet it is important that you transcendent the gunas, that you live a life which leads you beyond the gunas, these manifestations of Maya. So understanding these Gunas is essential.

The **tamas** is that which is sleeping. It is a powerhouse of energy, but it is in a slumbering state. All the tamas energy is the matter in itself. When you put a seed in the earth, the seed is going into the darkness. It is an ignorant state, but yet the seed is aiming for sattva, for flowering and giving fragrance. So there is sattva hiding in the tamas state, in the sleeping state of the seed.

Krishna says that none of the gunas are higher or lower, they are there, and eventually you need to transcend all of them. If the tamas stays tamas and does not aim for flowering, then it is not complete. So know the deep roots and nourishment in the darkness of tamas, but aim of the flower of sattva.

Rajas is the seedling that moves up through the soil and penetrates the earth, which has the courage to face the rain and thunderstorm. Rajas is the bravery of the seed coming out of the safe and nourishing soil. Rajas is the rising, striving and aiming for the flower. In the end there is the flowering and spreading your fragrance as sattva.

Every essence of tamas in your being should aim for sattva. But know that nothing is higher or lower. Tamas is the dark place where the seed grows deep roots, but the seed aims for sattva.

Know that all this is there, from seed to flowering, and yet there is beyond. There is a divine principle which is causing and leading this. Knowing the divine principle is crucial. See this process as Maya and Leela of life, and from that know the divine principle. Maya is not separate from the divine, it is the manifestation of divine. But do not limit yourself to Maya. Know the divine principle, and when you know that, you are beyond the gunas and beyond the Maya.

In this way you would be a true devotee and would thus come close to Krishna. When a true devotee comes close to Krishna, Krishna starts living in the heart of the devotee. And when Krishna comes, **Radha** comes along, and when Radha is in your life, your life is beautiful, your life is a divine love, a divine gratitude. Aim for Radha and Krishna in your life.

It is the blessing of Radha which will bring devotion and the blessing of Krishna with which you will know and practice the devotion. Call for Radha in the form of love and call for Krishna in the form of consciousness. The union of divine devotion, love in the form of Radha and divine knowledge in the form of jnana, that is who you are.

If you find all this knowledge too complex, then just fall in love with Radha. Fall in love with and be a devotee to Radha, be a devotee to love and beauty. Then love and beauty will guide you to Krishna. Sometimes this knowledge is too difficult to understand. Do not get overwhelmed, it is fine. Trust in love, trust in beauty and it will lead you to Krishna. Radha will lead you to Krishna.

Most of the gopis did not receive this knowledge. It is Arjuna who is receiving this knowledge. So, did the gopis not reach to divine liberation then? Of course they did, because Radha guided them through love, devotion, beauty and surrender. Only this, surrender, devotion, beauty and love is enough. This will guide you to Krishna. Radha guided so many gopis to Krishna, to this knowledge, to this understanding. Krishna came from within them, from their own heart and guided and gave them this knowledge. So if you find this knowledge too complicated, it is fine. Invoke Radha, call Radha and she will guide you to Krishna. She will show you the path to Krishna. She will show you the path to divine consciousness. Trust in love and beauty and it will guide you to devotion, and devotion will lead you to Krishna.

Now Krishna says, I am the **Ādibhūtā**, I am the **Ādideva**, I am the **Ādiyajña**.

I am the Ādibhūtā means, I am the ancient spirit from which all spirits come, the divine consciousness, the ocean of conciousness from where all spirits come in form of drops and I am that from where all souls are born.

I am Ādideva means, I am the ancient divine from where all the divine manifestations take place. This is the absolute consciousness from where every imaginable divine manifestation anywhere comes.

I am the Ādiyajña. As we described earlier, yajña is where a selfless action, a total enquiry or your meditative act becomes a yajña, and I am that original Yajña of the existence, what the scientists called Big Bang. The yajña is taking place in form of Big Bang from where the universe is taking birth. I am the Ādiyajña, I am the Big Bang from where this universe has taken birth. And not only this universe, but many universes like this has taken birth from that.

This is an invitation for you to the divine
To be in love with the divine
To be in devotion to the divine
Transcendent your limited life in service of the divine
You are welcome
You are welcome
This is an invitation to the divine.

Chapter 8

Beyond Life's Fleeting Sands, the Eternal Sea

By now Arjuna is getting a little more confident. He is asking questions. He asks, my dear Krishna, oh great Krishna, please enlighten me. Please tell me what is Brahman, what is Adhyatma, what is Karma, what is Adibhuta, what is Adideva?

Krishna explains, and with his explanation begins what I call the chapter of Vedanta, on the knowledge of deathlessness or **transcendence of death**. This part on death carries the essence of the Tibetan Book of Death from the Tibetan buddhism, the knowledge about the moment of death.

Now we come back to Arjuna's question about Brahman, Adhyatma, Karma, Adibhuta, Adideva and Adiyagya. Krishna says, understand what is **Brahman**. Brahman is then described as the ultimate state of consciousness from where all consciousness has taken birth.

Instead of imagining and trying to understand what is

Brahman, Vedanta went another way, trying to see it through the two ways previously mentioned. One way is the exclusion, diligently seeing what is not Brahman, like body, thought, emotions, identification with any state of consciousness, identification with any of the gunas, identification with any imagination or projection, identification with emotions, with any form, whatever we can imagine, whatever we can think of. Any identification with any kind of form is not Brahman. When we see this we also see that everything, whatever we can imagine, think or feel is bound to dissolve with death. What remains is Brahman. When everything is taken out, what remains is Brahman. This is how it cannot be imagined by thought, how it cannot be thought by thinking. This ancient technique of asking "who am I" is the key to know Brahman.

The Buddhists have been calling Brahman No Self, giving no description at all. But that is like saying, "we cannot imagine it so we will not even attempt". But one should attempt. Try to see, feel and imagine infinity, and when you attempt this, when you aim for imagining infinity, you will realise the limitation of the thought, of the emotions, of your perception, of you as a limited self. And with that realisation comes a total surrender, and in that moment Brahman reveals itself.

Brahman expresses itself in our consciousness as is-ness, as being, as seeing. In our limited body-mind-self Brahman reveals itself as seeing, as being, as is-ness, as knowing. Resting in that state of is-ness, of knowing, of consciousness, of attentive awareness is a door to Brahman.

In this chapter Krishna says, that it is your divine right and your duty in this life to know Brahman. Because through you the whole existence knows Brahman, because you are Brahman, you are the absolute manifestation of Brahman in this body and mind. Without knowing this, you are confined to your conditioned habits, thoughts and your limited self, but with knowing it you are a liberated being. So Krishna instructs Arjuna saying, oh Arjuna, know Brahman. Do not stay confined to body and mind. Know.

Bhagavad Gita has been seen as the highest text of Vedanta along with the Vedanta Sutra and Mukhya Upanishads, because Bhagavad Gita gives the motivation for you to know and walk on the path to ultimate liberation.

Liberation is the peak of consciousness, and it is your reality, Krishna says. Do not settle for anything less. Brahman is your reality. Know the Brahman. By knowing Brahman all illusions drop, the grip of space, time and matter drops and you are free, you are a liberated being.

Krishna gives the insights in Bhagavad Gita so gently, in such a poetic way in the middle of the battlefield. I doubt it has ever happened in such a way before. These insights have been the secret teachings available to few but Krishna makes it available for all through Bhagavad Gita, and that too in such poetic and easy to understand way.

The challenge with this knowledge is that without the practice of yoga and the call of devotion, it is difficult to know, and ideas like "I am not the body" start to form. The realisation of it does not happen, it remains an idea. With such identification one tries to distance oneself from worldly duties, responsibilities and actions and one try to suppress one's karmic expression.

To know and understand this knowledge you need the preparation of yoga, of meditation, of devotion, of Karma Sanyas Yoga, Sanyas Karma Yoga. Only after this understanding is there can this knowledge be given and received. Only after seven chapters, Krishna introduces deeper insights to Arjuna.

Then Krishna says that walking on the path of yoga is **Adhyatma**, going towards Ātman, because the day you know Ātman you know Brahman. The day you move towards Ātman you know Brahman. So instead of speaking about Brahman, Krishna is guiding towards Ātman or leading you to understanding your inherent nature. This is the path of Adhyatma, the spiritual path, Krishna says. He is not talking about any doctrine, that one needs to convert others or preach about it, he is simply saying, walk on the path of Adhyatma. When you walk on the path of Adhyatma a transformation will happen, and with that transformation your karmic imprints start to dissolve, dissolving your illusion of a limited self.

Arjun's insights are now getting clearer and he is beginning to understand. Then Krishna goes deeper into the Vedantic way of **seeing everything as Ishvara**. See this body as Ishvara, see this mind as Ishvara. Because everything has come from Ishvara and will dissolve into Ishvara. That is how Sāṃkhya describes it, that everything originates from infinite and eventually melts back into it. As everything originates from and dissolves into infinite, do not see anything as separate, "see everything as Brahman", as Adishankara says. As Krishna said earlier, Yogamāyā is also me, this limited self is also me, in a slumbering state but yet it is me. So see everything as Brahman, see divine in everything, see everything as a manifestation of divine. Everything is a manifestation of divine aiming for a conscious manifestation of the divine through devotion. This is another insight of Vedanta.

The first of the two Vedantic insights is through diligent exclusion, going deeper and deeper and seeing that I am not this, not that either, not this, not that. This second way is through devotion. Everything is Ishvara, everything is divine and everything is aiming for conscious manifestation of divine through devotion. All that is manifested is going towards the Ishvara, the conscious manifestation of divine. This way goes through Ishvara, through God. Ishvara is a beautiful expression of the word divine and God. Everything is Ishvara, everything is aiming for Ishvara and you go on the path to Ishvara through devotion, through surrender, through love and through seeing the beauty in everything, seeing the beauty of Brahman in everything

These are the two insights or the two ways of Vedanta. The finest and deepest of the understandings ever on this planet, because if the diligence of negation is difficult for you, if looking inwards and seeing "not this, not that" is difficult, then look outwards and see that everything is that and aim for Ishvara.

With this insight Krishna says, Adibhut, all the spirits come from me and all the spirits dissolve in me. Adidev, I am the ancient divine source of all.

Here I would like to put light on **devotion** because devotion is a core theme of Bhagavad Gita. No matter what you do, whether you do self-enquiry, whether you do yogic or tantric practices or you meditate diligently with dedication, it is the devotion that makes the difference. So understanding and knowing devotion is the key, because devotion purifies the heart, devotion takes you from love to absolute love, to ananda, to bliss, to the purest form of love. Devotion gives you courage, trust, honesty and sincerity without which there is no possibility of any yoga becoming successful. It is the heart of all yoga. That is why it is important to understand, know and live devotion.

Devotion is the highest and the greatest and the deepest form of love. With devotion the limitedness of life, of I, of karma, of conditionings starts to melt and dissolve and the purity of love starts to flower and the fragrance of love spreads in one's life as bliss.

There are many **expressions of devotion**, many ways a devotee lives the devotion or dedicates himself or herself to devotion.

One way is through listening, **sarvana bhakti** we call it, the bhakti of listening to the glories of the divine. Like a lover likes to hear stories of the beloved, the devotee loves listening to stories of the divine. Through listening to stories on the life of the divine the devotee is understanding, feeling, knowing and connecting with the divine, seeing the glory of the divine, listening to the glory, devoting all senses to the divine through hearing and seeing. Wherever you hear about your beloved, you pay attention, you hear the songs. Listening to Bhagavad Gita, for example, whenever Krishna is mentioned, the attention is raised and a smile comes on the face. That is the devotion of sarvana bhakti, listening from the heart, not bringing the mind in between with thinking, analysing and reasoning. Logic and reasoning has its place, but not here. This is a matter of heart. Love, joy, gratitude, bliss, and surrender is the nature of the heart. Allow this nature to manifest in your life through listening through the heart. When you have this love, this purity in your heart, you will see the beauty. You will see beauty in everything everywhere, and when you see beauty, you see Krishna, and when you see Krishna, the path to Ishvara, to ultimate liberation is filled with joy and celebration.

But the bhakta is not interested in liberation. The bhakta is happy just listening to stories and songs about the divine, listening and seeing the beauty and getting drenched in that beauty love and bliss. The beauty is the divine. That is the way divine reveals itself to the bhakta. It has always been said that if you want to find the divine, Ishvara, look for it in the heart of the bhakta, that is where he lives. So make your heart pure. Invite divine into your pure heart and it will come, it is bound to come. If your heart is pure it is there already.

Another way devotion expresses itself is through **kirtana bhakti**, dancing and singing songs of the divine, getting drenched in the songs and dancing along with the music of the divine. The moment you hear the music of the divine, your feet start to move and your heart starts to dance and sing. The kirtana bhakti allows you to sing and dance in the presence of the music of the divine.

Then remembrance, **smarana bhakti**, remembrance, remembrance. When Buddha left this planet, his last words were samyaksmriti, right remembrance. When many of the great saints left their body, their last words were remembrance. In the world we tend to forget. We forget and whatever is in front of us takes our attention and pulls us in that direction. And by the time we realise what happened a lot of time may have passed, a lot of years may have gone by. Long time passes by like this for people, their whole life is gone without that remembrance, many lives even.

The major role of the guru, the major role of Krishna in your life is remembrance. And that is what Bhagavad Gita is, it is a remembrance. Why remembrance? Because divine is our inherent nature. We not need to acquire it, only to pay attention to our original self.

In the east there was no concept of doctrines and dogmas. In the east dharma is the very existence itself and dharma is about bringing back attention to your original self, to your very existence, sanatan or that which is eternal.

So remember, but how?

Begin remembering as gratitude. Gratitude is the best way to remember, because the moment you tap into gratitude you are bound to remember. You are bound to remember that this life is limited to a certain number of years and will eventually dissolve. Pay attention to the gift of life in all its blessings and difficulties. No matter how difficult is your situation, you can still find something to be grateful for.

Remember that the path to divine is the way to transcendent this life and beyond. This is remembrance. It is the key, so it is called smarana bhakti.

Another expression is **pada seva bhakti** which is serving the feet of the divine, surrendering your ego, surrendering your I. In modern times there is so much comparison, envy, jealousy, competition and fixed ideas of how one should look and be, that the self-respect, self-esteem and self-love is not there. Due to lack of these aspects the surrender does not happen and the rituals of touching the feet of master or just totally surrendering to the feet of the divine is not there. If there is self-love and self-respect, surrender comes very naturally, that "I surrender this ego to you and there is nothing of me and only divine lives in me through you". That is pada seva which is gratitude. It is the greatest form of gratitude. Pada seva is the way, is the centre of devotion. If you are not able to surrender your ego, then no matter how pure your heart is or how blissful you are, the ego will still be waiting for the moment you are weak or in distress, where it is bound to come back. So guru is the way to divine and divine is guiding to guru.

Here, because Arjuna is totally surrendered to Krishna, this knowledge is being revealed, this knowledge is being given. If that were not happening, if there were no transformation, then that flow of love, that flow of blessing, that flow of life, that flow of jnana or knowing could not take place. So this is pada seva bhakti, which is at the centre of all forms of devotion.

Another expression of devotion is **archana bhakti** which is worship through rituals, like puja and mantras. The same way you take care of yourself through showering, wearing nice clothes and taking good care of your body, the same way you take care of the beloved through rituals, through shringar or creating beauty with ornamentation and flowers. That is archana bhakti, worshipping through rituals.

Rituals are essential. We do not see rituals, but they are everywhere. When you wear specific clothes, that is a ritual. Why do you not wear your pajamas to a business meeting? You are wearing a suit because that is the ritual. If you think that rituals are superstitious, that is completely stupid. Rituals are part of life. In the Bhagavad Gita, Krishna is sitting and giving his knowledge and Arjuna is receiving it at the feet of the master. This is a ritual. Rituals are everywhere and they are key. Archana Bhakti happens through rituals, worshipping through rituals. For example making good clothes for the form of the divine. One can also imagine the form of divine through visualisation, letting your visualising abilities flower. When Albert Einstein was asked, what he would tell to children of the future, he said imagination. This is imagination. Imagine the physical form of the beloved, of divine, of Krishna and worship that physical form. See Krishna and Radha in love, see the beauty.

Another expression of devotion is **vandana bhakti**, expressing devotion through prayer, through mantras or through your meditation. As Krishna said, dedicate your meditation practice to me, dedicate your life, dedicate your daily routinc, your daily rituals and your daily actions to me. That is vandana bhakti. Kirtan is a form of vandana where you express devotion through prayer and singing, it is vandana and singing together. The deepest form of vandana is when you meditate for the beloved, for Krishna, when you are living every moment to the fullest, and when every moment you are remembering. That is the greatest vandana, that is the greatest prayer one can offer.

Mantras are helpful because they bring your remembrance back, because there is so much distraction from all around. But at the heart of all vandanas is that you dedicate your action, your selfless action, dedicate your prayer, dedicate your meditation, dedicate your self-enquiry to the divine.

And then **dasya bhakti**, serving the divine. Do your action as serving the divine. Do whatever work you do in service of the divine. You are as a das, the one serving in total devotion, like Hanuman. Shri ram bhakt Hanuman is the greatest of the dasya bhakti. He is dedicating everything to shri Rama. Dasya bhakti is considered one of the highest forms of bhakti because in this expression there is selflessness and therefore no room for the limited self to form roots, for the Maya to form roots in you. Even Hanuman who is a great enlightened being, a fully liberated being, he is in dasya bhakti. So imagine what heights we are speaking about. When Krishna talks about his greatest devotee, he says, it is the one who is a realised being and yet serving. The most glorious of all bhakti is the dasya bhakti, when you are selflessly serving the divine, without any doubts, without any limited I. Through that the infinite starts to serve through you. The infinity start to serve the humanity and the world through you. You become a messenger of the divine. You literally become a hand of the divine. Being a hand of the divine by serving is dasya bhakti.

Another expression of devotion is **sakha bhakti** which is seeing the divine as brother, as friend, as beloved, as lover. For Radha, Krishna is the beloved, and Arjuna and

Krishna are there as two brothers and friends. This is the sakha bhakti, and in the sakha bhakti you are one, there is no separation. In every aspect of your life, you are giving. The joy of this bhakti is in giving, because a friend or a beloved is one who gives without asking. So giving, giving totally, giving, giving, giving, giving, giving, giving, giving. That is sakha bhakti. And at the core of this bhakti is the purity of friendship, the purity of love, the purity of is-ness.

Centuries back Buddha said he will return as Maitreya. It means he will be back as a sakha bhakti practitioner, one who is devoted as a sakha, as a friend, as a brother. The masterhood will transcend into friendship. This is sakha bhakti.

And then there is **Atmanivedana bhakti** which is total surrender, absolute surrender, absolute total surrender to the divine. First in love, in devotion, and when the infinity starts knocking on the door, then having no fear, just letting go completely. If your bhakti is true, then infinity or Ishvara is bound to come, Krishna is bound to knock on your door. That will surely happen. But at that moment, if one is not surrendered, if one clings to pleasures, to misery or to identification with ideas and conditioned thought patterns or if one is identified with the limited self, then the seed remains a seed and will never see the sky. No matter how difficult it seems, at that moment do not cling to anything, just totally surrender to divine. And the seed is bound for the journey of ultimate flowering, the thousand petaled lotus blooming and blossoming. This is Atmanivedana bhakti.

Atmanivedana bhakti is to be practiced every moment, because at the moment the infinity knocks your door, you are bound to slip due to your ideas. So many satoris happen to people, so many little samadhis, but not full liberation. Why? Because Atmanivedana bhakti has not been lived.

Atmanivedana bhakti is the key to living because it is your preparation for the moment of death. Without this, without bhakti you are not prepared. This is why Krishna is constantly emphasizing bhakti. All these different expressions of bhakti is a preparation.

In modern times spirituality has become split into several branches, one ideology based and dogmatised, another pseudo scientific and utilitarian, like meditating for tranquility or better sleep and a third is commerce based, as material experiences are no longer enough and we now crave for spiritual experiences. This is what is taking place in modern times. In the ideology based spirituality has been converted into some kind of idea, where rather than practicing and living it, one can just feel superior in perceiving oneself as a bhakta, as a great yogi or something else. In the so called science-based spirituality you can lose weight, you can have a better sleep, you can meditate and release your tension. And in the consumer based spirituality you can fulfil your hunger for spiritual experiences.

All of this is fine, but do not be limited by it. Religion has a place, commerce has a place and science definitely has a place. But you, your destiny is divine. You who are reading this, even if after thousand years from now, whosoever is reading this, you are not for this. You will not be changing spirituality into just one more spiritual experience, you will not be using spirituality just for good sleep and you will not be restricted by some fixed ideas and ideologies and confine yourself to that. You are a free, liberated being. Know thyself, know thyself, know thyself.

This was a short introduction to bhakti. Bhakti is something which can only be known by a heart full of gratitude. So fill your heart with gratitude and bhakti will come and knock on your door.

Now Krishna says, that all this is great, but at the time of death you will forget about it. If you are not practicing it daily, then at **the moment of death**, whatever you have paid attention to in life would be the focus in that moment. If fear has been your theme, then most likely the fear would be the focus at the moment of death. If greed has been your theme, then most likely greed would be the focus at the moment of death. If devotion is your focus, then devotion would be there at the moment of death. Brahman is the highest state of consciousness, Krishna says, but at the moment of death you are not likely to fall into Brahman, because you will not be remembering. Death is such a strong shock to the whole system that you are bound to forget. Whatever your life has been focused on, that is exactly what will be there in that moment. If you are limited by habit, then your death will be in a state of whatever habits you have been in, like habitual thoughts. Your mind has formed impressions, karmic impression of habits and thoughts. That is bound to be your death. If your life has been focused on chasing new exciting or pleasant experiences, then you will be scared, because now you cannot do that anymore. You will be scared of dying. And if you are living in a life of identification, of attachment to different ideas, routines and material possessions, then in the moment of death you will be holding on to everything. This will be very painful because death is pulling in one direction and you are pulling in the opposite, so you will become like a spaghetti. It is going to be very painful.

Krishna says, attaining the divine at the time of the death is the key. He then gives a **yogic meditation technique for the dying**. Krishna instructs this way; at the time of death rest in the place where your eyebrows meet, deep inside where you derive your self from. In that sense of self, imagine me in the divine form and surrender yourself to that. Then from that go on to Brahman, the infinite self, the infinite is-ness. In that state devote yourself, surrender yourself to the infinite. Surrender your breath, surrender your life force to that. Let your life force, your breath go into that.

It is exactly the central place between the eyebrows, behind your forehead. Neither move out nor in. Neither seek outwards, nor seek inwards. In that state of balance which is beyond all the gunas, beyond tamas, rajas and sattva, rest, rest, rest and let go. Let go while remembering, samyaksmriti. Remembrance of Brahman, remembrance of the infinite self, and if that is too difficult then remembrance of the divine self of Krishna. Devote yourself to that and let go into that.

This is the meditation technique Krishna gives to achieve deathlessness. It sounds easy now, but in the moment of death you are bound to forget it, so it is good to practice it while you can. Integrate it as a practice along with other practices of self-enquiry, meditation and selfless action. And practicing this technique, as an insight, you are bound to reach to total liberation and absolute love and trust. Trust, absolute love and total liberation is at the other end of the death, so trusting that is the key.

Now Krishna says, that if you do not practice this and understand what takes place in death, then at the moment of death you are bound to get identified with whatever state of being you are in.

Right now you are in the body. Everybody thinks of themselves as body, but when the sleep comes, then nobody is body and everyone is sleep. If you are body and you think, "this is me", then what happens to you during the sleep? Where does that me go? In the sleep you are identified with the sleep and there is no me left, only sleep is left. The same happens in the moment of death, you are bound to get identified with whatever state of consciousness you are in.

For example, if you are in a state of fear, then you are bound to get identified with whatever form of fear and misery is there. With death the individual mind gets weaker as the brain which was house to the individual mind dies. At the same time the collective gets stronger, so if your stream of consciousness is falling into fear, then most likely this will lead you to the experience which could be translated to hell. Do not go there.

Over time you build a karmic momentum and most likely that will decide your state of conciousness in the moment of death. When you are tired you fall asleep, but when your body is not there, mind is not going to fall into sleep as body is not there to be anchored into sleep, so the mind and the consciousness experiencing the mind will fall into whatever state your karmic impressions are leading you into.

The same way you are identified with the body now in the wakeful state you will become identified with the sleep, you will become identified with the loss of body and brain in the death and the same way you are likely to be identified with the state of misery resulting from karmic impressions collected overtime - and that is hell. Do not go there. Start preparing for the journey now, through devotion, through selfless actions, through meditation and through self inquiry.

If you have been living a good life, a life of joy, then at the moment of death you can also get identified with joy. Joy is not an ultimate state so you will still need to take birth again to be able to reach to Ishvara. So do not be deluded by that either and do not end up there. Krishna says, there is place of joyous gratitude and thereby the great birth will be waiting for you.

Take birth and reach to me again. Come back to me again, learn this knowledge and practice devotion till you reach the divine principle.

In the Brahman state you are free. You are free to take birth or not take birth, you are free to manifest or not to manifest. You are free.

Krishna also stresses the importance of **Aum** on the path. Breathing with the sound of Aum. Connecting your breath with the sound of Aum is very helpful in the daily life as well as in the moment of death. Start practicing it now, do not postpone it for the last breath.

Krishna emphasises that your path is to become a liberated being. Do not settle for anything less than that. Aim for the great liberation. Aim for the infinite self and go for it. In this life itself.

Krishna inspires you to do your daily action with the divine spirit of devotion, as a liberated being. Whatever action you do, do it in the spirit of devotion and surrender. Here Arjuna is standing in the battlefield, so Krishna tells him, stand upright and fight your battle with the divine spirit of total devotion. Do not hesitate. Do not let yourself be deluded by doubts. Lead your battle to victory in that same spirit. Do not fall victim to fearfulness or helplessness. Do your dharma.

Chapter 9

In Every Heartbeat, Hidden Secrets as Ancient as Time

Krishna calls this chapter the **raj vidya**, the royal secret. Why does he call it that? Because in this chapter he introduces worshipping and devotion. We need to understand that worshipping came after the Vedas and Vedanta. In the Vedic school there is yajña, but worshipping the divine in human form or idol form was not there. That came after the Vedas, and Krishna is introducing this knowledge of worshipping and the knowledge of karma, the law of karma. It is just a short introduction on karma, he will elaborate more on that in the later chapters, but as we introduced devotion in the previous chapter, in this chapter we will speak a bit on **the law of karma.**

Here, Krishna says that he is the ultimate reality. By this he does not mean in the human form. He clearly say that those who see me in my human form, my mortal form, are limited by their mind and their thought. Worshipping the Ishvara, the infinite consciousness, which is the origin of all and in which all will melt and disappear, that is what Krishna is calling for.

With the power of devotion to Ishvara, you can transcend everything in your life. All the karmic past can be transcended, your future karma, all your present karma can be transcended. By devoting and dedicating yourself through worshipping to Ishvara, to Krishna, you take charge of your past, present and future.

Krishna says, bhakti or **devotion is the greatest of all paths**. Why is that? Because if you have bhakti in your heart, if your heart is pure and open to receive to love, beauty and devotion, then your life has a very strong foundation of purity, courage, surrender and intensity. With this you can walk on the pathless path or the path of karma yoga, the path of Vedanta, self-inquiry or jnana. Or rather than paths it is a journey. Krishna is very clear that it is a pathless path as all the paths are intertwined, and whether you meditate, do self-inquiry or selfless action, devotion is the key. The basis of your journey is devoting your action, devoting your meditation, devoting your self-inquiry, devoting your daily life to the divine.

Devotion is at the core of everything, and devotion is the highest of all. Bhakti is the highest. There is no translation of bhakti in English. When we read the word devotion in an English dictionary it has a different meaning than bhakti. This is the reason I clarified the meaning of devotion in the previous chapter, as meaning bhakti and the nine gunas of bhakti - plus more when you add gratitude and compassion. With gratitude, compassion and purity of heart through the nine gunas of bhakti, you create a very strong basis for your spiritual journey.

Krishna then says, devote every aspect of your life to me,

and **your devotion will be received**. Your devotion will be received. Any offering you give to me will be received. Any offering given with a heart of devotion will be received. Whether you know rituals or not, whether you come from a very difficult past or have you a life of difficulties, misery and poverty, whether you are educated or uneducated, whether you are high born or low born, there is no distinction. With a heart of devotion everyone has equal access to Krishna. Without a heart of devotion many things matter, but with a heart full of devotion, love, surrender, gratitude and compassion Krishna is available to you, Ishvara is available to you, the great divine infinite consciousness is available to you.

As we discussed in earlier chapters, the divine is available to you as a friend, the divine is available to you as a guide and as divine light, as guru, as your inner master guiding you on the path, protecting and guarding the spirit in you. All of this becomes possible because of your devotional heart.

With **a heart of devotion**, life will have a different meaning. In your actions there will be a flowering of passion, purpose, beauty, serenity and meaning. Meaning is bestowed upon you and your life. Finding devotion in your heart and dedicating this devotion is the key to all yoga. It is the key to all paths. It is the key to the royal pathless path. When you dedicate every action, every every food you eat, every act you do, every decision you make to Krishna, to Ishvara, to the divine infinite consciousness, then your life becomes magnificent. This is the power of devotion.

We need to understand that that one is affected by **the law of karma**, as it is described in more detail later in the book as well as in other ancient text. The law of karma is complex, but with the guidance of Krishna we will do our best to put light on it. So, what is karma? Krishna describes it as cause and effect. A misunderstanding happens when karma reducing to the simplicity of crime and punishment, meaning that you did something which you will be punished for. That is absolutely not what Krishna says. Krishna says, cause and effect, action and reaction.

This **action and reaction** takes place in many different ways. For example, when you have a thought or when you do an action, straight away a reaction takes place, exactly at that moment. A kind of energy forms in your body, and that energy has an effect. If you have thoughts of gratitude, feelings of gratitude, then that very moment you are rewarded with serotonin. In your brain there will be dopamine, a great release of wonderful happiness, of joyful hormones in your brain, which then changes your neural network. You will have more clarity in your feelings and in your thinking, and because of that there will be more clarity in your life. From this your actions will be different, and those actions lead to the future. The reaction comes now. This very moment you are rewarded by the effect of the thought you have and the action you do.

Do not think of this effect as something small. The effect is big. It is scientifically proven that the hormones of love and compassion affect you here and now. It affects your health. Serotonin and dopamine affect you here and now, immediately after release. They shape how the neurons interact and affect the chemistry in the brain. If we look at the energetic system, your thoughts has energetic effects on your body, on your mind, and on your life.

This is the reason Krishna previously said, do not judge a monk or a sannyasin who is meditating full-heartedly in devotion. That action of inaction is the greatest form of action. See that. The same is the case when you do every day your life as a yajña, devoting everything to the divine. That has an effect energetically, and those ripples reach to the world and to your life. The first reaction happens instantly, and the second reaction happens over a period of time. This is how the law of karma works.

When you learn something consistently, you will be rewarded for it in this very life. Whatever education you take, this very life the effect of that will come to you. Whatever good deeds you do for your body by keeping it healthy, for your mind by keeping it sharp, and for your heart by devoting and surrendering it to the divine, this will have effect this very life. That action-reaction is going to happen in this very life. In this life you get rewarded.

This is how to build your life with the growth mindset. Wherever and whatever situation you are stuck in, do not limit yourself to that situation. The law of karma is in your favour, and you can change your life with this. Whatever you feel, whatever you visualise, and whatever action you do, it all has an effect. If you are supporting somebody, then that very moment you will be rewarded by your own brain and body.

The negative thoughts and negative karmas also have effects. If you have a "poor me" or victim attitude, a miserable attitude, thinking that you have no options, that you are bound by your past and your circumstances, then your brain will become shaped by that, and your life will take form like that. This is the law of karma. This very moment you are affected, and over a longer period of time during this life you will be affected.

Now we will explore the **sanchit karma** or accumulated karma. This is a little more complex. See, whatever actions and habits you havc accumulated settles in form of conditionings in your body and brain, and not only there, it also settles as karmic impressions in your spirit. These karmic impressions go dormant and take time to reveal themselves or open up. They stay in seed form and get ignited in the later part of your life or in the future lives. A big part of sanchit karma from the past is in a dormant form. Scientifically you see it in form of genetics. You have many genes from your ancestors, but the epigenetic is also at play, which means that genes that can either wake up or stay dormant depending on the conditions. There is a genetic structure of your spirit, which is formed over lifetimes, which can be in either dormant or awakened form.

The karma which is in awakened form is called **prarabdha karma**. Prarabdha Karma is what is in awakened form right now, in this time of your life. You are receiving that karma. There is a freedom in this though. You are not just a victim of that karma. No, that is not exact. Krishna says, in this very moment you can respond to the prabadha karma through your attention, through your consciousness, through your awareness. When you respond to it through attention and awareness, by meditation or by being present, then you have a choice to either change it or take charge of it and lead it. This choice is available. But the choice is only available when you have consciousness to respond to it through meditation, when you have devotion and courage to respond to it through bhakti, or when you have the strength of selfless action and you take responsibility. With that you can change it. So with yoga you have ability to chose how to respond to the karma coming from the past in form of the awakened prarabdha.

Now, this is the karma, how it is now. The actions you are doing now will shape your agami or future. And in the same way as described for the law of karma, the future comes both now, later during this life, and in the future lives.

See this, and start from this very moment, when you are reading this, start from this very moment with the good deeds. Start transforming. The greatest of all deeds, Krishna says, is that you offer every action, every thought, every emotion in the service of the divine, in the service of meditation, the service of yoga, in the service of selfless action and self-inquiry.

Krishna also says, **the liberated being is free from karma**. Not that the law of karma is not affecting the body and mind, but there is no one left to receive the karma. Everything is devoted to the divine, and living in that, divine is living in that being directly. This is how you can be free from the law of karma.

Aim for it through self-realisation. Aim for knowing Ishvara and being one with Ishvara. It is your destiny and your birthright. Claim it, go for it. Do not be limited by your conditioned self which has been conditioned through which country you are born in, which body you are in, which family you are born in, what education you are having, what kind of actions you have accumulated in this life in previous lives. Do not be limited by that. Aim for the total liberation, aim for the highest liberation. This is who you are.

Krishna is there, full-heartedly guiding you as a friend, as a brother, as beloved, as a divine God. In all forms Ishvara consciousness is there, nurturing you and helping you. Be devoted to this and worship it in all forms. Worship it in form of worship, worship it through your meditation, worship it through your selfless action, worship it through self-enquiry, worship it through every act of the day. When you go to sleep, fall asleep into it, and when you wake up, wake up into it.

As Krishna says, all beings come from me, and I am present

everywhere, but I am not in the awakened state in everyone. Your journey in this life is to reach to the awakened state of me in yourself, that I become awakened in you. Through this awakening, you dissolve into me once and for all, and there is no separation between you and me. This is the heart of Krishna's message.

Knowing this will open your life to a new journey, to an adventure you have never seen before. This adventurous journey to divine is absolutely worth it. Without this journey, Krishna says, you will stay in darkness and ignorance. The Yogamaya rules your life, and you will stay bound by the gunas you are living. You will stay bound by the illusion of the Yogamaya, and most likely you will end up either in experience of something that could be described as heaven or hell created by Yogamaya, depending on your karmic impressions. Pray that you go beyond heaven and hell, and if it does not happen in this life, then take birth again to be able to walk this path.

Krishna states with certainty that because this message is reaching to you, then this very life it is happening. So aim for it, aim for it. Do not let illusions guide your life. Walk from darkness to light. With this light, your life will transform.

Krishna also says, whatever you dedicate your life to, that kind of manifestation will happen in your life. If you dedicate your life to a certain desire, like having money, that desire will start manifesting in your life, provided you work for it. If you constantly feel like a victim of your life, with an attitude of "poor me", then your life is bound to go into that direction, into creating more misery. If you live a life of abundance, prasad or gifts and action, then that will shape your life. So aim for me, Krishna says, aim for me and then you will receive everything else as a blessing.

If you do not aim for the highest liberation, dissolving in

Ishvara, then your life will be dependent on and limited by your body, mind, conditionings and the law of karma, whereas if you aim for and devote your life to the greatest divine, then a divine hand comes to help you and guide you from darkness to light. Walk the path from darkness to light. Ishvara, Krishna is there with you, helping you, guiding you and supporting you this very moment. Trust and let go into the devotion to Ishvara, to Krishna.

Now Krishna states, that when you worship with all your heart, with all your devotion, then even a flower or a leaf that you devote to Krishna will be received. Stand in front of a stream and give a flower as offering or when you wake up in the morning put a flower in front of the statue of Krishna, but this must be with all your love and devotion, with full heart, then **your devotion will reach to Krishna**. Remember the nine gunas of bhakti? With the deep feeling of these gunas, place the flower and give it to Krishna, then it will reach. Krishna is indirectly sharing something akin to a technique here, because there is no technique for devotion. Devotion is a feeling, a way of life. It is not about techniques, but indirectly Krishna says here, that even a flower or a leaf, even a dry leaf offered to me in full devotion, carrying the deep feeling of the gunas of bhakti, this reaches to me. When you worship for merits, that also reaches, Krishna says, but I am happy when you worship in devotion. When you worship in distress, that also reaches to me, but I am joyous when your devotion or bhakti reaches to me.

When the Krishna consciousness, the Ishvara consciousness, awakens in you, and you devote that consciousness to me, this is the highest form of bhakti. That is why Hanuman is considered the greatest of the all bhakta, why Radha is considered the greatest. Radha is an awakened being, an enlightened being, a liberated being who is totally dedicated and devoted to Krishna and in love with Krishna. The highest form of bhakti is Radha's bhakti to Krishna, Rukmanij's bhakti to Krishna, Lakshmi's bhakti to Vishnu, ma Shakti's bhakti to Shiva. This bhakti is the highest form.

So yes, Krishna says, your worship and your bhakti does reach me. When you ask for merits, material gains or other things in your life that reaches me, when you call me in distress that reaches me and when you call me in love just for the sake of devotion, that also reaches. But the highest bhakti is when the consciousness in you awakens, when your heart is drenched in love and in devotion. That reaches to me and I am delighted. At that moment I celebrate. For my celebration, devote that bhakti to me.

This is Krishna's guidance to bhakti or devotion. This is the **raj vidya**, the royal vidya, raj yoga, the highest of the high, because you have direct access to Krishna. The heart of the devotee has direct access to Krishna, and even a flower from a devotee, even an offering of sweets or food from a devotee reaches him. It is not about what you give, whether you get up every day and do puja and rituals for the aim of siddhi. You may be seeing it as your job as a priest or in the temple, or you may be worshipping for greater benefits in your company or in your life, or you may be in total distress. All of this does reach the divine, but it stays limited by your state of mind.

What touches divine profoundly is the sincerity, the heartfulness, the love, the compassion, the devotion, the dedication, the surrender, and the deep feeling of the bhakti gunas through shravan, kirtan, smaran, padaseva, archana, vandana, dasya, sakha and nivedana, through giving your very essence to Krishna.

So know yourself. Devotion is the heart of this chapter. See this last part as your inspiration and read it over and over again for guidance to the path.

Chapter 10

Echoes From the Infinite From Which We Never Part

The best moment of life or the peak of life is for most sages the moment of death. The death of the body is now coming and life is reaching to its peak. When their disciples, devotees, students or fellow travelers ask a last message the from these sages, the greatest of the Zen masters, they all give the same message: remember, **Samyaksmriti**.

The world pulls you in all directions. A recent book, "Nudge" by economist Richard H. Thaler describes nudging, a process of influencing people's decisions through making changes to their environment. Another modern book, "Thinking Fast and Thinking Slow" by Daniel Kahneman shows how our mind constantly gets tripped up by cognitive shortcuts. Both authors won a Nobel Prize in economics for their work. These books show us how our mind is prone to get influenced in many ways, how our attention can easily be diverted into something mundane which has no value at all. This is how we trade our diamonds for stones. We trade the precious moments which are diamonds in our life for something stupid, and in this way the diamond of life is missed.

The **humility** that comes from the understanding that our mind is prone to being influenced and distracted is very important. If this humility is not there and we arrogantly think that, "now I got the knowledge of Bhagavad Gita and now I will meditate every single day", that is not going to happen. "Now I have understood the path and now I will walk the path", that will not happen either. Why? Because our mind can be easily moved and influenced, and our thinking is full of shortcuts or cognitive biases. That is what chapter ten is about.

Krishna says, understand the **importance of remembrance**. Importance of remembrance through devotion, importance of remembrance through love. There is one form of remembrance that comes from discipline and practice, but Krishna guides to the path of remembrance through love. Love is Krishna's way. Krishna is not imposing discipline, that you "should" or that you "have to". He says, by being in love, by being in devotion remembrance will flower in your life. And when you remember me, when you remember the divine essence, you will save a lot of time and energy which otherwise goes in sheer wastage. See how much of the time of the day goes only for the daily maintenance. Eight to nine hours sleep, two to three hours of self care, house chores, shopping and other things, two to three hours of cooking and eating. How much time is left? Around eight to ten hours maybe. And then we have also have to make a living. That is why Krishna says, make your whole life as a remembrance. Do not only take one hour out for meditation, make your whole life for remembrance.

Krishna emphasises that the moments which are lived,

the moments devoted in love, those moments are yours, everything else is just in preparation for those moments.

Let us just say we have a good and healthy life and live up to ninety years. Out of those ninety years the majority of our life goes into making a living and daily maintenance. And in these days phones have added another time-consuming factor. So we do not have much time. Therefore this chapter is of utmost importance as it shows us that through devotion, through remembrance of your beloved, through remembrance of the divine you can gain mastery and control over your life. This chapter guides us to **take back control of our life**.

The whole commerce industry is after your attention, we know that. And you need to make a living, so you need to trade. You trade your life energy and attention just to stay alive in this big collective system. Your attention and life energy is limited.

In the previous chapter Krishna showed that, when your actions are selfless, devoted to divine and you live a life of meaning and purpose, then your life starts to transform. In this chapter the focus is on **remembrance**, and Krishna says, the easiest is to remember me and see me as the source of all. And that is how it is. Divine is the source of all. It is through divine everything manifests. Through divine this life has manifested, this universe has manifested, all the dimensions of this existence have manifested. And this manifestation is not limited to the universe. All the living beings, all the human beings come from the divine. The divine may not be awakened in them, it may be totally asleep, but the origin of all is divine. The divine manifestation in us is in the life energy, in the life force. Our life itself is the manifestation of divine, that which takes us forward, which brings evolution to the species. We have evolved.

Look at the modern research, the industrial revolution, the capital revolution, technological revolution and now AI developing. All that is the life force. That life force in itself is the divine which is taking us forward. But only the individual has the ability to awaken the divine. Without the awakening of the divine the life force still moves and flows forward, but the awakening of the life force brings the manifestation of the divine directly in your life.

Krishna then moves on to talk about **excellence**. He says that he is the eagle among birds, he is the samved among Vedas, the great among the great, the sun among the celestial beings. This is a poetic expression of excellence, but it is very important to understand why he is saying that. The life energy seeks excellence. In us and in every other form it seeks excellence, so when we seek excellence in our life we are close to Krishna.

When you make a cup of tea, if you make it excellent, Krishna says, then I am that cup of tea. This is an expression of excellence. You can bring Krishna in your life through excellence. Whatever job you have been given or have given to yourself, do that job excellently, to the best. If you write then write the best, if you design then make the best design. When you make the bed in the morning, make it excellently and when you clean the house, clean it excellently. Krishna says, I am the cleanliness you have brought in your home.

Some of the best artists, film directors, musicians, actors, and leaders know this secret. They know that when they are in their excellence they are closer to the divine. The taste of the divine in the excellence keeps calling them, keeps bringing insights to them, keeps giving them energy to take things forward. Some of the brightest innovators were motivated by this. Steve Jobs wanted to take humanity forward by bringing personal computing to everyone. "We don't get a chance to do that many things, and every one should be really excellent", Jobs said. He did not know that by saying that he was coming closer to Krishna.

This is the beauty, that whatever field you are in, whatever you do, you can bring excellence to that. When making a simple cup of tea, make it excellently. Find the best ingredients and make the tea with love and awareness. Take care of your body and carve it like an artist carefully carves his sculpture. Let your prana shine. The vitality of tapas should shine from your prana and the aura of prana should radiate through your presence. Shape your personality to excellence with utmost care, developing kindness, courage, humility and sincerity. When you do that, Krishna will manifest in your life.

A step deeper would be reaching to excellence in every aspect of life and devoting the process and action to divine. By devoting your action to Krishna, you awaken the Ishvara principle in form of bhakti.

Krishna describes a **meditation technique** for awakening the Ishvara principle: Whatever you do, **anchor your mind into Krishna**. Anchor your thought, your feeling, your emotions into me, Krishna says. If you are cooking food, cook it as if I would be eating it. If you are designing clothes, create them as if I would be wearing them. Anchor your mind into me. If you are designing a building, make it as if I would be living in it. If you are making a movie, make it as if I would be watching it. If you are building a nation, build it for Krishna to come and live in. If you are leading a nation, lead it as if it was given to you by Krishna to take care of for him. When you anchor your mind with the remembrance of Krishna, your mind is not going here, there and everywhere. You are directed towards and for Krishna. With this, a new flowering of creativity and life energy will manifest.

In the Vedic yajña you give ghee and herbs to the fire. In the same way **give every breath to Krishna**, put the sacrifice of the breath into agni, into the fire of divine life. How would you do that? Pay attention to every breath, be aware of every breath and let every breath be love. Let every breath be an expression of love. How is that possible? If Krishna is there, he will take your misery and your pain away and give happiness and joy to you. In the same way let every breath take away the pain and misery from this world and give back happiness, joy and gratitude. When you inhale, take all pain and misery as Krishna would do. When you exhale, give back joy and happiness. This is the breath. Devote the breath to Krishna. Here, my Krishna, this breath is for you. Pay total attention, have total awareness and give total love to that breath in that moment.

So anchor your mind in Krishna and devote your breath to Krishna. With this Krishna's devotion would manifest in your life and gratitude for life will flower in you. And when you are grateful you cannot miss remembrance. Remembrance and gratitude goes hand in hand. When you are grateful you remember the people you feel grateful for.

These days there is so much me-me-me. The consuming energy has become so powerful that we want to consume anything and everything. If Krishna came today, people would want to consume him through retreats and meditation classes, through spiritual experiences and life experiences.

Our mind has become so rigid, timid and tiny that even if infinite came in our life we would change it into an experience. This is the path to hell, Krishna says, because then there would be no more open doors left for you. Then you have shut the last door of Krishna in your own face through your limited mind. Do not do that to yourself. Let gratitude flower in your life through every breath, and through that gratitude,

Krishna's presence will manifest in your life. Krishna in you will awaken, Radha in you will awaken, love will awaken, consciousness will awaken. Consciousness is Krishna and love is Radha. Wisdom is Krishna and celebration and joy is Radha. So when wisdom and bliss awaken in your life, imagine how your life would become. When consciousness and love awaken in your life, imagine the change in your life.

Your journey in life is to awaken consciousness and love through remembrance, through remembrance of Krishna.

Krishna warns of arrogance. He points out not to see anybody as lower than yourself or think yourself superior and special because you are on this path. You do not know the other person's journey. You do not know from where the other person is coming. But do appreciate wherever you see the awakening of Krishna in form of excellence, in form of love, in form of consciousness. Welcome that in your life.

Krishna later says, I am the fame of the famous, I am the deceit of the gambler. What he means here is that he is knocking on everybody's door in different ways. So welcome even the difficulties and challenges in your life, seeing that Krishna has brought this in my life for me to overcome and become a bigger person. See it in this way,

Through these insights, through this remembrance you start worshipping Krishna with your breath, with your action, with your mind, with your energy, with your prana, and through this worship your life will become a blessing. Through that blessing the door to ultimate liberation opens, the door to great liberation opens. Devote and dedicate your life for this. That is Krishna's message.

When you have the flower of devotion in your heart, you are protected, Krishna says. But if you do not have that, it is likely that you will get influenced or nudged into some direction where the door to Krishna is not accessible. Or where you start thinking that it is not accessible. Or you simply forget it in your daily routines or ups and downs of life. So remembrance, samyaksmriti as Buddha calls it, is important. Remembrance, remembrance, right remembrance. This is the right remembrance.

Krishna does not say be disciplined, wake up every day four o'clock, practice and that is the way you will remember. He does not impose anything, he only says, love, gratitude, and see divine in everything. See and seek divine in everything. That is it. A very simple message, as simple as it can be. This is beauty in simplicity. The simplicity of love, of gratitude, of seeing the divine and receiving the divine in your life and sharing the divine through your life.

This is chapter ten, the most important chapter as this chapter will change your everyday life into worship, into prayer, into a path to the divine. It will change every breath of yours into yajña, it will change every act of yours into service of the divine. This is the core chapter. Whenever you feel away from the path, this is the chapter, this is the guide to turn to. Come back to this chapter and start from here again.

Chapter 11

Infinite Realms Where Wonder Traverses

Chapter 11 brings the focus to **the bigger picture of life**. Our mind tends to become very focused on what is happening right now. Immediate problems, immediate gratifications and whatever we are busy with take the attention. The mind tends to have a very narrow focus, either on goals or whatever your job is, and the stress of the job takes over. Or you are preparing for an exam and that exam becomes the most important thing and nothing else matters. Or your bills, your ambitions, your daily life routines and habits takes over.

In my life this changed around age 7 or 9. I was studying in the Indian education system that has tests every month, and I was so engaged with these tests. All my focus was dedicated to it, but one evening I was standing on the roof and looking at the sky and wondering about the vastness of life and its creation in form of our universe. A mystical force took over which carried the blessings of silence and infinite, and a sense of inner freedom was available as attention was no longer limited to the mundane.

Lets **see our universe with a fresh perspective**. There are billions of stars in our galaxy. And those billions of stars could have a multitude of planets with life. Billion is a huge number, approximately 200 billion stars are there in our galaxy only. And then there is approximately the same number of galaxies in the universe, in the visible universe. Universe and visible universe. Imagine that for a moment. Billions of galaxies and billions of stars in each galaxy. Then hundreds of planets in those galaxies where there could be life. This visible universe has so much. Billion is a huge number. And see the distance between. How vast is the universe. I am not talking about beyond the universe. The modern research says that this universe is just one of many universes and we do not know how many or infinite universes there are.

This is where we are, but we limit ourselves to something very tiny. It may look very big, and for you it is definitely big. I am not doubting there are very important things that need to be done, or that you may be facing real problems in your life. It may even be the biggest problem anyone has ever faced on the planet Earth. But **from the perspective of the infinite**, then where is today? Where is this body? See how tiny we are in comparison to the vast universe. Alexander wanted to conquer the Earth and that is 2000 years ago. After that how many Alexanders have come and gone? How many countries and kingdoms wanted to expand all over the world? How many Napoleons and Genghis Khans have come and gone? From the perspective of the universe it does not matter how much fame, wealth and so-called success you gather.

See where you are from the perspective of the universe. You may have the worst illness, you may be facing the most difficulties imaginable, you may be struggling with poverty, or you may be facing a battle like Arjuna. Everybody has battles in their life, but see it from the perspective of the Universe.

Next is Arjuna's longing to know the infinite and Krishna's answer to that. Krishna says, I will give you eyes to see because you cannot see it with these eyes.

What Krishna says is that we confine ourselves through our eyes. Our eyes are our limitation. Our eyes are designed to see the matter, to see distance. They are not designed to see the infinite. It is our **divya chakshu** we need for connecting with infinite. This is also called the ajna chakra or the third eye, and we all have it. We receive it from the infinite at the inception of consciousness. It is the inner eye. We are all blessed with it, but it is sleeping, it is not awakened.

What exactly is divya chakshu? When you have the power of visualisation, when you imagine something, what can you imagine? You can only imagine the finite. Try imagining the vast galaxies, it would still be finite. You can imagine the biggest planets, still it would be finite. You can see the largest of the suns, still finite. The greatest of the black holes, still finite. The largest galaxies, still finite. Multitude of galaxies, still finite. One universe, still finite. Multi billion universes, still finite. One year, finite. One thousand years, finite. One billion, one trillion years, still finite. All of it is finite.

Divya chakshu gives you access to infinite. Not only will you be able to see, you will be able to know the infinite. But how does it open? It opens when you have seen the limitation of your body and mind by testing it, by taking it to the furthest, by attempting to reach through this body and mind and realising that it cannot reach. Through meditation, through self-enquiry, through devotion. Through imagining the infinite in you.

Take time out and **try imagining infinite**. See the vastness. Try it now when you are reading this. Close your eyes. See and feel hundreds of light rays going through you and reaching to the infinite. Follow along those light rays to the infinite. Let those light rays guide you to the infinite nature of the Ishvara, of Krishna. Then from the furthest place in the vast existence, let the a multitude of light rays come towards you but not reaching you because you are not there. Only infinite is there.

That which has no end, as Arjuna describes it. What I see has no end, no beginning, no middle. It has no place to limit it. It is limitless. This is very important. No end, no beginning, no middle. No then, no now, no future. Absolute is-ness, absolute is-ness spread in the vastness of the universe, spread in the vastness of this existence. Absolute is-ness turning inwards.

Your life energy is awakening and the divya chakshu is opening so the vastness, the is-ness, the infinite becomes directly accessible to you.

This is what Krishna is blessing Arjuna with. And Arjuna sees it. He does not only see the infinite, he also sees time and movement of time. Time is the only thing in this universe which has no beginning and no end, which is visible, and we can feel. We cannot feel the infinite, but time we can see moving day in and day out. The sun rises, and the sun sets. Every moment moves, and in every moment there is the dance of life and death.

Hundreds of thousands of people born on this planet, and this is just one planet in this vast universe. Hundreds of thousands of people dying every day, every second somebody dies. This very moment somebody died. This very moment somebody is born. This very moment somebody is going through death. Your death is bound to happen. It is just a matter of time. Time is moving.

Arjuna sees the death of everyone. He sees the Kauravas dying, the Pandavas dying one day. In this divine form of Krishna, he sees all that. He sees his own death. He sees death. He sees movement of time, he sees movement of life, he sees the vastness of this life. This becomes so intense and so vital for Arjuna. He falls onto the ground with tears in his eyes and says, thank you, thank you, thank you. He has great gratitude to Krishna.

Krishna then says, fight your battle. And Arjuna sees. What is this battle, the greatest of the battles, in the vastness of this universe? Nothing matters after seeing this. And Arjuna gathers all his courage and says, yes.

Arjuna is feeling overwhelmed by the experience and asks Krishna to bring him back. Such is the vastness of this universe, Krishna in his magnificent form. Arjuna's mind is conceiving the infinite manifestation in form of thousands of hands, life and death, life in every dimension, past, future and present, everything happening at the same time. That is exactly what it feels like when infinite knock on your door, when you know infinite for the first time.

So aim for the divine infinite to reveal itself to you. You are born limited and without this you will die limited. Come out of the limitedness of this life. Transcendent your life and transcendent your death. Before death knocks on your door, know the infinite nature of divine, know the infinite nature of Ishvara. Merge into this infinite nature. That is your destiny.

Do not let your **limited life stories** define your life. That is what was happening to Arjuna. He has a name that is bound to the body, he has a title through his work, he has created a life story and narration for himself. And that narration is his life. Krishna shows here, that the narration you have created for yourself is nothing more than sand and dust.

Imagine how many grains of sand there would be if you counted all of them, on the beaches, in the deserts and so on. Even more than this is the number of stars in our own galaxy only. Astronomers calculate that approximately 10.000 stars exist for each grain of sand on the Earth. That is how vast this universe is. And you are limiting yourself to a little life story, of where you are born, which body you got born in, what life experiences you have, a story which is has come about mostly by coincidence. You identify yourself with life experiences as Arjuna was doing. Arjuna was identifying Krishna with his body and his title.

Now Arjuna says, I am so sorry that I was identifying you with your name and title. I was limiting you to your physical form. What I see now is sheer vastness and absolute infinity.

It was not physically Krishna became like that. Arjuna did not see Krishna physically like that. All the people who come and sell their agendas through religious books may tell you otherwise. What Arjuna is seeing here is the vastness of this universe, Ishvara spread in all the dimensions of this existence, in multiple universes, in multiple dimensions.

Imagine, this body have trillions of cells. Your neuronal network can cover the whole Earth, and your blood vessels can cover the Earth multiple times, they are so vast. If you counted all the cells in the body, how many cells would that be? Imagine the amount of electrons and photons in each of these cells, in your body itself. There is a whole universe in there. Every cell has its own universe with photons and electrons. Your body has an immense intelligence of its own. All the cells are moving in harmony but you think you are doing it. You think the stories you tell yourself, of who you are, what your name is and so on, you think that is the reality. That is like stories from a children's book that you read in your mind. You are creating narrations in your life, that "I am this and I am that and I am going to work and getting ready every day". This is a narrative you are telling yourself.

See from the perspective of Ishvara. See from the perspective of Krishna. Open your divya chakshu. It is your divine right to open your divya chakshu. Do not be limited by the physical eyes. Do not be confined by the senses. You are vast. The whole infinite nature is sitting inside you, ready to awaken, ready to enlighten.

Krishna then says, **my devotees will reach to me**. My devotees will reach to me. The one who is in full devotion reaches to me. So be that devotee of Krishna and know yourself, know yourself. Do not be limited by your body and mind.

Krishna says, the one who engages in my pure devotion, free from any speculations, who is friendly to all living beings, certainly comes to me.

What does Krishna mean by that? Krishna means not to carry animosity for others. Be in kindness and compassion. No animosity, have kindness and compassion. No speculations, no ideas, no narration, neither about yourself nor about the divine. Know. See the purest nature of divine in its infinite self. And devote every action, every breath, every moment, every cell of your body to the divine. That is the devotion. A devotion full of compassion, of clarity and awareness. These are the three aspects Krishna describes in this shloka. Selfless action, self-enquiry, awareness through meditation and total devotion, full of compassion, full of surrender, that is your path to Krishna.

Let go into the infinite nature of Ishvara. Let yourself dissolve in the infinite nature of Ishvara. It's your divine right to reach to total liberation. Aim for that, work for that. It's your duty. Self-realisation is your duty.

The ripples of enlightenment are felt by the whole universe. Alexander can conquer the whole earth but the universe would not even know which Alexander on which planet. But one enlightened being and the universe awakens. One enlightened being and the existence awakens and knows. That is your divine right. That is what you are born for.

Devote yourself. Devote yourself. Do not make it into an ambition. This is your divine nature. Devotion, devotion, devotion. Ambition is something else, it is a word of the mind. But a seed aiming to flower, fighting the thunder and the storm and rising, rising, rising towards the sun, towards the sky, that is the courage which Krishna is invoking in you. That flowering is your divine right, that fragrance of the flower is your divine right. Flower and kiss the sun. Let your consciousness spread its wings. Let your heart reach to the divine. Let your life energy and your whole self see the vastness of this universe, the infinite nature of this universe. Let your divine nature spread in this universe, in the vastness of this existence, the infinite nature of this existence. That is who you are. That is who you are. That is who you are. And Krishna is your way through devotion. Let Krishna bless your life.

Chapter 12

To the Melody of Love, Heart Begins to Swing

Chapter 12 may be the most read chapter of Bhagavad Gita because it gives exact descriptions of how one should be if wanting to be close to Krishna. The greed of wanting to be close to Krishna makes people read this chapter, not the longing but the greed. Longing is beautiful, but greed is a misfortune.

I love that Arjuna is so sincere in his seeking. He is also innocent. He is brave, innocent and sincere. These qualities are loved by Krishna. Here, Arjuna asks with all sincerity, is it better to worship the form or the formless?

It is a good question. Should one worship Nirguna Brahman or worship the form, all the devas and devis, all the gods and goddesses. Which is better?

Krishna says, all the forms are mine.

This is beautiful. He is not answering Arjun's question

straight away. He says, what matters is the devotion, the heart of the devotee, the depth of the devotion. If you worship without devotion, it does not reach anywhere.

With this, Krishna is again pointing to devotion. But what devotion? A devotion beyond conditioned thought patterns, beyond ideas, beyond how and what. A devotion which is totally dedicated, a devotion which is pure at heart, a devotion with the deep expressions and feeling of the gunas of bhakti. A devotion beyond thought, with all the senses alert, this is what Krishna is pointing to.

Then Krishna describes the difference between **worshipping the formless and the form**. He says, worshipping the formless is difficult, almost impossible.

Why does he say that? To Arjuna he can say that worshipping the formless is better because Arjuna has experienced the formless. But if you have not experienced the formless, then whatever formless you think of would come from your mind, from your own form, from your memory, thought, imagination, projection and so on. You cannot imagine or perceive the formless through the instrument of thought, idea, perception or conditioned mind. Hence worship of the form is easier, simpler. If you aim to worship the formless without knowing it, there is a high risk of hypocrisy, a risk of going in circles and ending up with the arrogance of knowing it all without knowing anything.

Krishna says, set your mind and your heart to me in devotion and worship my form. Worship the beauty, the divine. Worship with gratitude, with all your heart. Worship, worship. Dedicate and devote yourself to selfless action. Give your every breath, every day, every action in service of the divine.

When you have tasted the formless, even for a moment,

worship formless. Worship formless. Then all forms would reflect the formless, the divine infinite Ishvara.

Body is a form, so take care of your body the way you take care of Krishna. Take care of your mind through developing a sharp mind. Have a pure heart through protecting your innocence and have a healthy body through yoga, pranayama and good diet. Take care of the form, worship the form and set your mind to the formless. See the formless in everything, in every aspect of life.

This is a magnificent clarification. Krishna is clearing the doubt in Arjuna's mind once and for all.

Now Krishna says, if you are finding devotion difficult, then do not let that stop you. You may have grown up in a culture where bhakti is not understood, and you only know love as romance from Pride and Prejudice or Hollywood movies. Maybe you do not know what bhakti is. In that case **take refuge in abhyas**, in practice. Practice meditation techniques, practice yoga, practice asanas, practice pranayama and learn different meditation techniques and abhyas. Do it day every day from early morning. Give your practice as much time you can and do it with utmost sincerity till you are blessed with bhakti.

Even when you are blessed with bhakti, still take care of your body by practicing yogic exercises, and still take care of your mind through meditation.

Krishna also says, take refuge in practice, but **devotion is the highest** and at the heart of everything. Let your heart dissolve in bhakti and it will guide you. When the love of bhakti grows in your heart, it becomes your guide, your teacher, your master, your guru. Rest in this bhakti. That is Krishna's message.

Now Krishna says that if you find it difficult to practice than **take refuge in seva**, do seva. Krishna does not say either or, perceiving it like that would be a misunderstanding. These are safety nets he is creating. If you are unable to go into devotion, then take refuge in practice because you would not be in a state of total devotion. Or take refuge in seva, selfless actions, serving the divine, serving in the service of the divine. Krishna explains that abhyas and seva are easier to start with.

They all have importance. Meditation has importance. Self-enquiry has importance. He is not putting one way higher or lower than others, but he does emphasise bhakti.

Why bhakti? **Bhakti is complete in itself**, and the heart of the bhakta is the abode of Bhagwan. No further reason is needed, but for the sake of the modern mind's understanding, let us look more into it. When you are on the path of self-enquiry, you need the intensity, let go, total surrender, trust, courage and compassion that comes from bhakti. If you enter self-enquiry without these qualities, then most likely your self-enquiry will become an intellectual pursuit, and you will be bound by your own mental gymnastics. The same can happen to selfless action. If the sincerity and intensity and totality is not lived through bhakti, then there is a likelihood that your selfless actions will quickly become limited. Then you are limited in that particular setting of your life and continuing in your habitual way of life.

In selfless action there is a **pitfall** of habit, and in self-enquiry there is a pitfall of intellectual gymnastics and feeling intellectually superior. And on the path of meditation, there is a pitfall of developing an ego as a great practitioner, as a great yogi, as a great meditator. What can rescue you from these pitfalls is bhakti, that is Krishna's message here.

If seva has been difficult for you, **take guidance from the guru**. Learn from the sages. Take instructions and follow those instructions.

Krishna is giving a **practical approach** here. Guru is your guide, seva is your path, devotion is your wings, and practice paves the way. Integrate it in your life, as a continuous process, day in day out, like a river flowing to the ocean.

Now Krishna describes some of the **qualities of utmost importance** for seekers.

He first highlights **compassion** saying, if you have animosity in you, if there is a lack of compassion in your heart, most likely the ocean of love is not available to you. Compassion and kindness are two of the very important qualities, and true courage is compassion. Compassion demands courage, that you are not limiting yourself to me, me, me.

In the spirituality of modern times, there are many retreats available with goals like achieving a peaceful mind, a better body, having great meditation experiences or spiritual experiences or in the pursuit of so-called enlightenment. All these are selfish motives, and with the selfish motives, your meditation cannot flower.

That is why in many of the ancient traditions like Buddhism, Jainism, Zen Buddhism, the core practice before anything else is devoting your meditation, devoting your practice for the goodness of the earth, for the goodness of humanity, for the goodness of all living beings, for the goodness of the future. You dedicate your practice, your meditation, your awakening in service of the other. This is compassion. With this thought, your focus and attention is not on me. It is on to the other, on the greater good, on the humanity.

With this foundation you can think of the infinite. If you are not even able to think of the other, how are you going to put your mind and heart to the infinite? Infinite is everyone, everything, all universe, existence in itself. If you are limiting yourself to your life, your experiences, your this, your that, your spirituality, your awakening, your meditation, your enlightenment, your ambition and all that, then how is it possible? If you are doing asanas, pranayamas and other practices for better sleep, for better metabolism and for better health, then you are limiting yourself. Of course, take care of yourself as taking care of the divine. That is self respect, that is self love. Take care of your body as a boat of divine, as a home of divine. That is the essence. But "me, me, me", this is limiting yourself. And no compassion flowers in that limitedness.

Then Krishna shines light on another important quality, **equanimity**. Now, it is very important to understand this. In a true state of equanimity, the joy is in the process as well as in the result. But the mind likes to jump to the result, to the fruit of the action.

Krishna also makes it clear through his actions that equanimity is not about becoming cold and aloof. When his friend Sudama is coming to see him after a long time, he is not cold. He runs without his shoes to meet his dear friend. If you see Krishna from outside, he may look like a person overwhelmed with the friendship and all in attachment. Krishna does not mean to be cold and unfeeling. He says, in equanimity you know and understand what you are experiencing.

Let us take emotions as an example. If there is fear in life, then understand it fully. Understand every aspect of fear. What is fear? How did it originate? What is the thought behind? How is it created? How does it take control of your life? If anxiety is ruling your life, then understand anxiety, how it is formed and what it is. You must study it and develop the state of equanimity with mastery of the anxiety, after cleaning every aspect of the floor of your mind. Do not just close your eyes, avoiding situations where the difficult emotions surface, whether that is greed, fear, ego, anger or any other emotion pulling you out of the state of equanimity. **Understand the emotions to the core**, and through that transcend them. This will make your mind clean and clear. Still as a clear lake on a full moon night, that is the clarity that must develop.

Krishna does not shy away from joy and neither from sorrow. He feels sadness and joy deeply. His sensitivity is at the peak. He is the peak of compassion. He feels deeply, yet there is a state of equanimity in him, yet there is a state of total surrender in his being. Silence resides in the deepest core of his heart. A **state of easiness is at the centre**, a state which nothing ever touched and never touches. There might be a storm of joy, celebration or meeting a friend on the surface, but at the heart is purity. Krishna does not shy away from any of these emotions. He does not pretend to be in equanimity with no experience of emotion. That is not the case. When he took the message of peace to Duryodhana, and they disrespected him, he did not shy away from showing his rudra rupa, his civilised anger.

Even though there is no action prescribed for Krishna, he is in the middle of the battlefield, fighting alongside his brother as a charioteer, or a driver as it would be in the modern times. Krishna is a prince, yet he has chosen to be a charioteer of Arjuna. This is tricky to understand. Krishna is in the state of **total effortlessness**. He is in the state of total ease. He does not say, be lazy, stay at your home and do nothing and only practice. No, absolutely not. Do your dharma, do your action. Follow your love, your passion, your purpose, your meaning in life. Do your selfless service for the divine. Devote your every breath, every moment in service of the divine. This is Krishna's beautiful message.

Do not let simplified translations affect you. See the complex nature. It is like a maestro orchestrating music. The nature of it is complex, yet it is the simplest. As complex as music, yet as simple as Buddha's smile. When the union of complex and simple takes place, the dharma happens.

Krishna says, the one who follows dharma is the highest, is my chosen devotee.

To be Krishna's chosen devotee, follow the dharma, welcome the dharma.

Chapter 13

Dualities Merge in a Dance so Deep

Chapter 13 is a chapter where science, psychology, philosophy, spirituality and religion meet. It is the origin of contemporary psychology. In the West psychology is a very recent science, but that is not the case in the East. Buddhism has done a great research on psychology and given a great understanding of it. Before that, Krishna himself introduced psychology as a science and as a knack. Psychology and philosophy is the essence of chapter 13. Here Krishna provides a scientific understanding of the nature of the being.

With the modern perspective, with the modern mind, if you have not been connecting to spirituality, maybe you are atheist and want to keep a very logical and rational mind, then this is the chapter you start from. This is the chapter which brings you inside. It is not about devotion. It is pure science, pure understanding of the human nature.

Chapter 13 starts with Krishna explaining **Kṣetra and Kṣetrajña**. Kṣetra is the field. This field can be the outer field of your life, of the world, your body. This field can be anything which is limited by space, time and matter. It is a field. And Kṣetrajña is the one who is living, experiencing and participating in this field.

Now here, as we enter into a deeper understanding of Kṣetra and Kṣetrajña, we begin where Krishna and Arjuna are. They are standing in Kurukṣetra. Kurukṣetra is the battlcficld, and they are in the middle of it. Krishna is very clear that there is only one rule of Kurukṣetra, to win. There is no other rule in the battlefield. You need to win.

The Kauravas and Pandavas are both in Kurukṣetra, aiming for winning, but Pandavas are not only in Kurukṣetra, they are in Dharmakṣetra too. That is the difference.

Everybody will be in Kurukṣetra sometimes in their life. There are battles to fight in everybody's life. If you are preparing for exam, you have to clear it, you have to win. If you run a business, you need to be successful, you need to pioneer and profit, you need to be excellent, produce the best products or give the best service. You need to innovate, you need to find the best technologies, you need to reach out. This is Kurukṣetra.

Krishna is not outside Kurukṣetra, he is in it. Bhagavad Gita is taking place in the midst of Kurukṣetra, and Krishna is aiming for winning the battle. He is not escaping from the battle, and he is not letting Arjuna escape either. Arjuna is going towards Dharmakṣetra saying, I am not participating in life and devoting my life to the inner. But Krishna says, no, you cannot escape Kurukṣetra, and Dharmakṣetra is not somewhere out there, it is always where you are, whatever stage of life you are in. Now, at this point in life you are here, in Kurukṣetra, and the rule here is very simple–fight and win.

Whatever you do in life, have a **growth mindset**, have a winning mindset. Be successful in whatever field you are. If you run a company, make it the best company, be at the top of your game. If you create movies, make something that will fascinate and amaze people even after 50 or 100 years. This is Kurukṣetra. Kurukṣetra is about leadership, team, collaboration, competence, and excellence. It is about growth mindset, success, and winning. There are no excuses in Kurukṣetra, and there is only one rule–winning.

Why is it Arjuna who receives the Bhagavad Gita and not Duryodhana or one of the other Pandavas? Because in Arjuna, there is a deeper instinct or power calling him to **Dharmakṣetra**. Arjuna is not only in Kurukṣetra, he is also in Dharmakṣetra, and the rules of Dharmakṣetra are totally different. Dharmakṣetra is about meaning, purpose, transcending and reaching to the highest consciousness. It is evolution, reaching to the deepest compassion, understanding interconnectedness of things, mastering purpose, mastering meaning in life. These are the rules of Dharmakṣetra.

Arjuna is a master of martial arts. He is the best of the warriors, yet the deeper phenomenon of Dharmakṣetra is much more powerful in him. That is where Krishna comes into the picture, and that is why Bhagavad Gita is given to Arjuna and not to anyone else.

Krishna will not only guide Arjuna in Kurukṣetra to help him win, he will also guide him in Dharmakṣetra and help him transform and transcend. He will help him attain to the highest state of consciousness, to the evolution of the human consciousness. This is Krishna's aim for Arjuna.

Krishna says, your action in Kurukṣetra does not come in your way, vice versa. If you escape from Kurukṣetra, following your instinct of Dharmakṣetra, there is a risk that you will fall into the **trap of escapism**. Do not fall into that trap. Stay in the battlefield, master Kurukṣetra, but let your mind, your heart, and your being reside in Dharmakṣetra. This is the beauty.

This is this chapter of **Dharmakṣetra and Kurukṣetra,** the conflicts we all go through at different times in life. You may have everything in life, be very successful, have gathered name, fame, celebrity status and have great wealth, but be very poor and totally lost in Dharmakṣetra, completely at the mercy of Kurukṣetra, completely in misery, completely bound by limitedness of life. That is where Krishna comes in your life and guides you to Dharmakṣetra. He holds your hand and says, come, let us go to Dharmakṣetra.

You may have a burning desire to know Dharmakṣetra, wanting to escape from Kurukṣetra. Kurukṣetra may be bothering you. Once again, Krishna comes in form of a brother, a sakha and guides you saying, my brother, your place is in Kurukṣetra. Krishna not only guides you to win in the world, he also helps you transcend and transform your consciousness while you are in the middle of the battlefield, giving you the greatest song of divine ever. That is the beauty of Krishna.

Krishna also says, see your body as **kṣetra** and see yourself as **kṣetrajña**. This is important, he says. Kṣetrajña is at the heart of the consciousness. Without kṣetrajña, without understanding of kṣetrajña, there is no understanding of kṣetra.

Science has dived completely into understanding kṣetra. Understanding the neurons, the endocrine system, the respiratory system, and the other organs. This science has only gone into kṣetra, whereas the meditators went into the understanding of kṣetrajña. They defined everything about kṣetrajña. Only the ancient Shaiv tantrics worked on the **interconnectedness of the kṣetra and kṣetrajña**, and that lineage is completely destroyed.

Krishna says beautifully, in me kṣetra and kṣetrajña becomes one. The observer is observed. The self becomes one. There is no duality. There is no difference between kṣetrajña and kṣetra. With this insight, there is a clarity, but without this insight, the duality prevails. And Krishna is not shying away from duality. He says, see and understand kṣetra and kṣetrajña. Kṣetra and Prakṛti, consciousness and matter, nature.

The pitfall of straight away going into "all is Brahman and everything is Brahman" is that you could break the interconnectedness of your body-mind and consciousness, you could break the interconnectedness of the kṣetrajña and kṣetra, observer and observed, by distancing yourself from ksetra. The truth is that, as a seeker, there is a difference in you of the observer and observed.

In the last shloka of this chapter Krishna says, the one who understands this difference is on the path to know me. He adds, but at core there is non-duality, and in Krishna all becomes one.

This is a beautiful insight, seeing the difference between observer and observed. Without understanding the difference between observer and observed, you can never reach to the point where observer is observed, what Krishna is describing.

But what exactly is **observer and observed**? It is the kṣctra and kṣetrajña in the inner.

In the inner you must **understand the self**, the nature of the self, how it is formed, and what consciousness is. Explore consciousness through meditation, through self-enquiry, through practice, through abhyas, through devotion, and through selfless action. With this you can understand the self.

Do not fall into the trap of greedily wanting to reach non-duality straight away. With that there is a high risk of getting identified with the illusion of non-duality or with the thought or idea that "this body is not me". Identification with the thought is not realisation. These are two different things. If you repeat, "I am that, I am that", know that this realisation cannot come from repetition.

This was a secret doctrine so that you first understand and master Kurukṣetra. On your journey to Dharmakṣetra, guru gives this knowledge to you and guides you to understanding of your own body, mind, thought, how the self is formed, what the self is, and the nature of the self. Guru makes sure you do not go into philosophical jargon without understanding your own body, mind and senses.

Here Krishna emphasises that one must understand the observer, know the observer. Let it be the awakening and transformation in your consciousness that guides you to the infinite nature of the Brahman.

The infinite nature of Brahman, you are that, I am that, everything is that and there is nothing but that, Krishna says. These are the great sayings, the Mahavakya's of Brahman Sutra, these are the Mahavakya's of Upanishads. You are that, I am that, all is that and there is nothing but that. This is oneness, when observer is observed, this is is-ness. It is the vastness, the infinite nature of the being.

You are infinite, you are infinite, you are infinite. Know thyself, know thyself, know thyself.

But do not be in greed of this. Understand Kurukṣetra, know being in the battlefield, know Dharmakṣetra, find meaning and find purpose in your life. Devote your heart in the service of the divine, devote your action to the selfless service of humanity for the divine. Practice, meditate and devote your meditation to the divine. Know thyself, know thyself. Enquire, seek to find who you are. Ask, who am I? Who am I?

What is the kṣetra Krishna speaks about? Kṣetra is all the senses, all the sensations, all the actions, all the actions and all the ways you take actions. It is your buddhi. Buddhi is usually translated as intellect, but buddhi is much more than intellect, it is that with which you have insight, intuition, with which you develop the clarity of seeing, of being, the ability to pay attention. That ability to see is buddhi. So kṣetra is mind, all the thoughts, all the emotions and the body with its instincts, its health and illnesses and every dimensions of the body with its birth and growth to its old age and death. This is the kṣetra. Understand this kṣetra.

Krishna says, when you understand kṣetra, you will know kṣetrajña. You would become aware of yourself in the process. You would know the consciousness. Because without the consciousness, there would be no kṣetra. And without the kṣetra, there would be no consciousness of the consciousness. With the creation of the existence, the consciousness is aware of the existence of the nature. And with that awareness, it is also aware of itself.

It is not that you are directly aware of the Brahman. If that were the case, then why even take birth? Why is Brahman not aware of Brahman itself? Taking birth is the way. The expansive, multi-dimension expression of your life is the way to know consciousness.

So when you know kṣetra, you would also know the kṣetrajña. And when you know kṣetrajña, you would know that kṣetrajña is not limited to observer, is not limited to kṣetra. **Kṣetrajña is infinite in nature**. It is the illusion of the kṣetrajña to be observer, to be drishta or bhokta, to be the experiencer or poor me, victim of this kṣetra. It is only because it is limited and time bound, space bound and matter bound. When ksetragya realizes that it is matter bound and space bound, it also realizes that it is infinite in nature. That very realisation happens at the samc time.

So do not shy away from kṣetra. Do not shy away from Kurukṣetra and Dharmakṣetra. Participate in life full heartedly with all your devotion, with all your action.

Krishna then says that there is something else you must be aware of. This insight alone is enough. There are some **characteristics you must not allow to develop** in you. He highlights what in modern psychological science would be called narcissism, being focused on oneself and feeling superior to others. Beware that you do not develop such traits, and also that you do not turn into a poor me, a victim of life to whom life happens without you taking responsibility, it is always somebody else's responsibility, and you are complaining constantly. This is ego. Krishna warns not to fall into the **trap of narcissism or victimhood**. This path does not reach anywhere.

Krishna also says, **do not be unkind**. Feel the pain of others, develop compassion and empathy. Do not become like a sociopath, non-compassionate and unfeeling. When you feel deeply, you feel the pain of the other. Have compassion and be forgiving. Krishna is highlighting the pitfall of not developing feelings and compassion. This is psychology thousands of years ago. With such clarity the psychology developed. Krishna clearly told not to go on that path, but **be compassionate, kind, and helpful** to others.

Krishna stresses not to be cunning, but **staying pure at heart**. Do not move others for your own gain, and do not hurt others. Be aware of this.

These are some of the important qualitites Krishna is mentioning–compassion, selflessness, seeing and taking care of the other, not hurting the other and forgiveness. Without developing these qualities you are bound to be limited to the self.

He also emphasises the quality of **expressing yourself**, what you think and feel, using the power of spoken word.

Yet another important quality is **serving**, guru seva, serving your master, serving your guru through selfless seva. Krishna emphasises this because in this you are close to the source. It is your door to divine. Take good care through service, through action, that is your door to divine.

Krishna also accentuates **purity of heart**. Develop the heart in its purest form. Let your heart be pure and innocent. There is great beauty in the innocence.

One more quality Krishna underlines is **mastery**, both of your body, instincts and senses. If you want to master the body, then wake up when you decide to, not later, and if you decide to eat a certain amount, eat only that and not more. Take good care of your body and master your instincts. With mastery of instincts, you can transcend to beauty. Without mastery of instincts, there is a likelihood that you will become victim of your own instincts, be moved by your own instincts. Master your senses. Do not be moved by them, do not be scared of them, and do not run away from them. So master your instincts, master your body, master your thoughts, master your communication, master your senses.

With this mastery, you are bound to transcendent what

Sigmund Freud called the pleasure principle, the instinctive seeking of pleasure and avoiding of pain to satisfy biological and psychological needs. You will transcendent all the phenomena which most of the world is moved by. Most of the world is moved by a few of these so-called principles. The pleasure principle, the survival principle, the needs and the ego. All the needs move you, as Maslow explains with his hierarchy of needs. And the ego also moves you.

With this mastery there is bound to be a transcendence of these phenomena which otherwise move you. Then you can be in the world, in the middle of pleasure, yet not be affected by it. You can enjoy the greatest success, yet not be moved by it. You would be able to take care of your needs without being moved by them. This is the power of this science or nayak as Krishna calls it.

Krishna says, **be aware of death, old age, sickness and pain** in life, the way Buddha was aware. With the insight and awareness of old age, with the insight and awareness of sickness, **humbleness** will grow in you. There will be humility in you. You will be connected to the suffering of the world, not arrogant in your own little world, in your own little castle above everyone.

Krishna is here emphasising **mastering the body and mind** and the **developing inner qualities** for walking the inner path. Today most people jump into spirituality either for better health, for being more peaceful or for spiritual experiences. In the ancient past there was emphasis on developing the right qualities. There was emphasis on mastering body, mind, senses and instincts. For example mastering the sleep instinct through getting up early in the morning, mastering the hunger instinct through fasting, mastering the instinct of body through asanas and pranayama, mastering the mind through overcoming laziness or procrastination, making your mind strong with that. Developing this mastery is essential on the journey of spirituality, on the great adventure of spirituality.

Understanding **the five elements** is also crucial for the inner journey. The five elements are the nature of the fire, the nature of the water, the nature of the sky, the nature of the earth and the nature of the wind. Understanding these five elements is key because through understanding them you understand this nature in yourself.

The **element of fire** can be of different kinds. The fire of longing, the fire of wanting to reach to your goal or the fire of anger. What kind of fire? Are you burning yourself in the fire of anger or hatred or do you have the fire of passion with which you find meaning and purpose in your life?

Is your nature flowing like water? Are you flowing with the **nature of water** in your life? Bruce Lee once said "be like water, flow like water", and some of the ancient texts of Tao also underlines this nature.

The **element of the sky** which comes from meditation, the elements of the flow which comes from trust and surrender, the **element of the wind** which comes from adventure and exploration, the element of the fire which comes from passion and longing, the **element of the earth** which comes from taking good care of your health and mastering your instincts. These are the different elements which together form the essence of your nature.

In ancient China the whole spiritual understanding was focused on these elements. The whole insight of Tao is understanding these elements because when you understand them, you understand your own nature, and when you know your nature you understand the kṣetra. By understanding the different elements, you will understand your inner nature. Knowing and understanding and mastering kṣetra is the key.

Then Krishna says, know, **understand and master your senses**. There are senses and there are sensations. The art of vipassana is about watching the sensations of the breath, both in the body and in the mind. The art of tantra is about senses and sensations, mastering your instincts and mastering your sensations. Understand and master your instincts and master your sensations. This is understanding the kṣetra.

But you can master your senses without mastering the dharma, the spiritual aspect. You can be very good with asanas and master your body without ever being present in any of the asanas, without ever tasting the spiritual essence in any of the asanas. The **principles of Kurukṣetra and Dharmakṣetra** also apply here. In the Kurukṣetra, your goal is winning, your goal is mastery, and in Dharmakṣetra, your goal is to know yourself, know your meaning and purpose, know your nature and devote your actions, that very service, that very meaning and purpose to the divine. Practicing an asana and mastering an asana is Kurukṣetra. But resting in that asana, dissolving in that asana, and devoting that asana to divine is Dharmakṣetra. That is the difference. Mastering your senses is Kurukṣetra, but devoting your senses to the devotion, to Hari, to Krishna, to Ishvara–this is Dharmakṣetra. The principles of Dharmakṣetra and Kurukṣetra also apply in the inner.

In the first part of this chapter Krishna gave the understanding of the outer aspect of Kurukṣetra and Dharmakṣetra. Here he is explaining the inner aspects, that mastering the kṣetra is key and devoting the process of the mastery to the divine is dharma.

Krishna says, when you devote yourself to dharma you are

bound to reach me. I will find you as a friend. I will reach to you as a guide. As he reached to Radha, Arjuna and all the Gopis.

There are great warriors on the side of the Kauravas, but what does it mean that they are great warriors? They are masters of Kurukṣetra. They are not masters of Dharmakṣetra. But when Kurukṣetra and Dharmakṣetra meet, you are bound to win. That is the secret of the Pandavas winning the battle, because Krishna is with them. Krishna is using all the principles of war in Kurukṣetra, yet he is giving Arjuna Bhagavad Gita in the Dharmakṣetra. So, when dharma leads Kurukṣetra what will happen? The truth is bound to win, the divine is bound to win. And it is your duty, your right and your responsibility that you master Kurukṣetra and you devote yourself to Dharmakṣetra. Both inner and outer. Outer we have described earlier, now we focus on the inner.

How can one **master the inner**? We have learned about the elements and about mastering senses and instincts. Now **understand the self**, know how the self is formed and master the self. Krishna does not discard the self, judging it as being bad, which is a misunderstanding in recent times. The self is part of you the same way your senses are.

Know how the self is formed, how any kind of identification is formed. Understand the self, and understand that there is identification. If you have to identify yourself with something, then identify yourself with values like compassion, kindness, purity of heart, full devotion and life affirmative principles. Identify yourself with these values, and let your values be expressed in the world through your actions, through your purpose and meaning.

Here Krishna clearly points out **what sends you on a journey away from divine**. The ego in form of narcissism as "I the superior, the one entitled to whatever I want", or "poor me, at the mercy of my circumstances, whining instead of taking charge of my life". Be aware that those characteristics do not develop in you. Be watchful that unkindness does not develop in you, that you are not being careless of others, focused narrowly on reaching your aim without any consideration for others. Be kind to yourself and be kind to others. Don't be deceitful and manipulative in order to reach to your goals. Do not cause pain to others. Be aware that you do not disconnect from the deep feelings, becoming unable to feel deeply. Have empathy and compassion for others. Know forgiveness, it is a core value. Learn to forgive yourself and others. Sincerity, purity of heart, clarity of mind, mastering of your body, mind and instincts, these are some of the values Krishna is emphasising. He is giving a key through these values.

And then Krishna says, **understand the different emotions**. Envy or jealousy for example. What is jealousy? Do you compare yourself with others? Do you see yourself successful only when your success is recognized by the world? Do you see the need of recognition in yourself? I think it is there.

Observe how fear, anger or greed arise in you. Understand envy, jealousy, hopelessness, sadness, distraction and the modern days' constant craving of dopamine through social media, games and series.

Understand this, know this. Use the discrimination power of your buddhi, your ability to see things with clarity. Use the attention power of consciousness, the power of awareness to know this.

Krishna instructs not to judge these phenomena as bad. See the self, but do not judge it as bad. See the self and the ego developing in the self, but do not discard it. Observe and understand, that is the key.

This is a chapter with very practical insights. If you forget everything else, at least remember the Kurukṣetra and Dharmakṣetra, the Kṣetra and Kṣetrajña.

What is kṣetra, and what is kṣetrajña? Kṣetrajña is the one who is experiencing, either as drishta, bhokta, karta or rogta. As drishta observing or witnessing everything. As karta doing. As bhokta living or experiencing and as rogta complaining and crying.

In meditation drishta develops. A sense of witnessing, a sense of watchfulness develops in you. You are watching the kṣetra. As a doer or karta you participate in the kṣetra, as bhokta or experiencer you experience the kṣetra and as rogta you complain about the kṣetra. Know these four different natures in yourself. Know the self, how it is developed. Understand the difference between kṣetra and kṣetrajña.

Krishna now goes a step ahead and says, in me there is no difference of kṣetra and kṣetrajña.

This is the peak of the Upanishads, the Vedanta, the highest knowledge. When the difference between Dharmakṣetra and Kurukṣetra disappears, when the difference between kṣetra and kṣetrajña disappears, only the oneness, the is-ness remains. This becomes your nature.

But do not be cunning and straight away try to jump to this is-ness. Krishna warned against that in the previous chapter. Do not fall into that trap, nothing such is possible. You would be totally confused. Where the point is Kurukṣetra you would be dancing in Dharmakṣetra, and when you need to be in Dharmakṣetra you would be in Kurukṣetra. The kṣetra as body-mind would overpower the kṣetrajña, and in an overpowered state you may lie crying "I am that", but you would be nothing but an illusion of body and mind, repeating like a parrot "I am that". Do not fall into that trap.

Yet it is your destination, it is where you will reach, it is your birthright, and it is who you are, your inherent nature.

Know thyself **where Dharmakṣetra and Kurukṣetra is one**. Look at Krishna and Arjuna, Dharmakṣetra and Kurukṣetra is one. Their lives are of purpose and meaning. Two brothers in the battlefields. Bhagavad Gita is manifesting, the highest and greatest of knowledge is manifesting, yet they are in the Kurukṣetra where winning is the goal. They are following the rules of the Kurukṣetra, to win, to win, to win. But what winning? Dharma is winning. The purpose and the meaning is winning. It is not their self that is winning, their ego that is winning, as Duryodhana. No, they are speaking about the illusion of the ego.

The same is with the **kṣetra and kṣetrajña**. "The observer is observed" as Krishnamurti put it, "witnessing the witness" as Osho said, "seeing is being" as Ramana said, "there is no self but that" as Buddha said. And as the Mahavakyas described it, "I am that, you are that, this all is that and there is nothing but that". This is your destination.

Here Krishna says, I am one, I am the Kurukṣetra, I am the Dharmakṣetra, I am the kṣetra and I am the kṣetrajña. I am that, I am that. This is beautiful.

After this realisation, your life will be new. There is no conflict. The misery cannot bind you. You are beyond life and death. Death is just a mere check post on the journey and nothing more than that. This is true equanimity. This is true equality.

Now, Krishna is moving back to **devotion.** He says, a devotee who is **practicing adhyātma** in daily life, who is on the journey to Ātman, that devotee is my highest, my beloved, my delight. Who is such a devotee? Radha is such a devotee, the great sages are such devotees, and Krishna is aiming for Arjuna to become such a devotee.

Krishna then delves into the **Ishvara principle**, the powerful mystical force which is in all of us, which is moving the whole evolution, which is at the beginning of the universe, which is at the end of the universe, which is in the middle, which was, which is, which will be, from where we have arrived, into which we will dissolve, from where all the universes are born, and into which all the universes will dissolve. Ishvara is all and everywhere. It is in all and every being.

All the mouths are his, all the hands are his, all the eyes are his, Krishna says. This is the Ishvara principle, and Krishna's expression of it is just a limitation of language. All and everything. The shakta calls it Har, the lovers of Krishna calls it Krishna consciousness, Krishna calls it Ishvara principle. It does not matter what you call it, what matters is what it is.

It is neither being nor non-being. Neither it is being nor it is non-being. So do not be limited by the non-being or no self. And it is not being either, so do not be limited by the being-ness of it.

The finite is part of it and all the infinite is part of it. The finite comes from it and dissolves into it. What comes from infinite is finite. All the prakṛti or nature is also infinite. Beyond the visible universe, there is invisible universe, and beyond that it continues to infinite. That is infinite. All the universe is infinite. In the matter form also.

But your perception is limited to the being or non-being. Your mind's perception is limited to either being or non-being. It calls something finite, and that which it does not understand it calls infinite. But perception is limited by the matter, time, thought and space. And Ishvara is it, yet it is not it.

Everything comes from Ishvara, and everything dissolves into Ishvara. It is in a sleeping or unawakened form in you. It is in the conscious and the unconscious, it is in the form of life and it is also in the form of rock and matter and the universe. It is in the form of life evolving. The evolution is Ishvara. The life is Ishvara, the death is Ishvara and in between is Ishvara. It exists in all, in everything.

And through you, Ishvara knows. Through your devotion, it awakens in you. Devotion awakens the Ishvara principle in you.

All the light, all that which is beyond darkness, comes from Ishvara principle. All the darkness is also part of the Ishvara principle. Everything you can imagine is Ishvara principle, is in Ishvara principle.

See that. Do not stay limited to your present thought, your present conditionings, your present habits, your present identifications, your present so-called self, your ego. Do not limit yourself to that. This limitedness is what Krishna calls ignorance. Do not fall into to the ignorance. Be the jnani.

Knowledge here means jnana, not accumulated knowledge in the form of data, information and memory. Jnana, knowing oneself, knowingness, is-ness, the knowingness of is-ness, through that know the Ishvara principle.

Know Ishvara principle through devotion, by melting and merging into it. Know Ishvara principle through selflessness, through dissolving the self which you have created through habits, thoughts and identification. Know Ishvara principle by dissolving the duality of kṣetra and kṣetrajña, Dharamkshetra and Kurukṣetra. Know Ishvara principle by dissolving duality. Reside in the non-duality of the Ishvara principle. Ishvara principle is the non-duality.

Brahman, that is Ishvara principle.

And in your life be aware. It is **awareness of the death** which gives you urgency. It is the awareness of the old age which keeps you humble in your youth. It is awareness of illness which gives you respect for the vitality of health. It is awareness of the pain which guides you to go beyond pain and pleasure to the Ishvara principle through devotion and jnana.

So know yourself and know the Ishvara principle. This is the heart of Gita.

Krishna describes it beautifully when he says, know the Ishvara principle as **purusha and prakṛti**, consciousness and matter. Know non-duality through duality, because Ishvara principle is too far from you to know. Understand the consciousness, live the consciousness, meditate to understand consciousness and live life to the fullest to understand Prakṛti.

Be in love to understand the love-nature of consciousness and conscious-nature of love. Dissolve in devotion to understand consciousness and stay rooted in action to know the prakṛti. This understanding is at the centre.

Krishna depicts the **nature of prakṛti** magnificently. Prakṛti is the manifestation of the three gunas, **sattva, rajas and tamas**. The whole next chapter is about the gunas, but I will give a short introduction to it here. See the gunas through an example. The seed in the darkness is in tamas. The seed fighting its way up through the soil with bravery and courage, ready to stand to the sunlight and face dangers of rain and storm, ready to grow and aim for the ultimate flowering is rajas. And the flowering and the fragrance of the flower is sattva. The insight which guides the seed from seed to flower, that principle is sattva.

Krishna says, I am beyond all this. He does not say that he is sattva. He says he is beyond all this, both sattva, rajas, and tamas.

Take away the darkness and nurture of the earth, and there will be no sattva. Take away the insight which guides the seed to reach, and the seed stays seed forever. Take away rajas, and the seed might never come out of the soil or will stay a seedling. This is the nature of the prakṛti. Understand this prakṛti in yourself.

Prakṛti manifests as **doer and deed**. Whatever action you do, that action will create a kartabhav, a bhoktabhav or dristabhav and quite often a rogtabhav, bhav meaning expression of emotion or feeling. That is the doer which originates from prakṛti. Prakṛti imposes this onto the consciousness in form of the doer. So, whatever you do is bound to affect the experiencing nature of the consciousness. At the core consciousness stays pure, but your experience of the consciousness would be limited to and by the doer and deed. It is in form of is-ness, and adhyātma is reaching to that is-ness.

So prakrti affects the experience of consciousness by giving it structure from the doer. From deed to doer, from experience to experiencer, from observed to observer. And consciousness affects prakṛti by moving it and giving it vitality with which it grows and expands. Understand and know this interconnectedness of purusha and prakrti.

Adi Shankar, Nisargadatta Maharaj and Maharishi Raman all put emphasis on how our identification or association with the properties of prakṛti limit us. **We limit ourselves** through identification with the properties of the self in form of karta or doer, in form of me and my or the one who holds or posesses, in form of identification with ideas, instincts, body, thoughts and emotions, and in form of observer or experiencer.

And beyond those identification, there is purity, pure being or **'no-self'** as Buddha called it. This is your destination. And through this you know the Ishvara principle, you know when observer is observed, when Dharmakṣetra and Kurukṣetra are one, when kṣetra and kṣetrajña dissolve, and non-duality shines in you.

Welcome to the Ishvara principle. It is your divine right. Ishvara principle has chosen you.

Know thyself, know thyself, know thyself.

Chapter 14

Nature's Rhythm, a Ceaseless Ebb and Flow

Krishna calls chapter 14 the **alchemy for the sages**. It is one of the most important alchemies to learn for the individual on the path of spirituality. It is a science that is very important in nation building, as well as in any individual's life, for succeeding in any field. This alchemy gives you mastery of Kurukṣetra. And if you learn it well, it will take you to Dharmakṣetra and help you transcendent your life.

Krishna says that with this science bad luck can never touch you, and with this science you can master your own destiny and become creator of your own journey. You can vision for and master your life, and your journey becomes smooth.

Krishna calls it a science, a knack and an alchemy. And a good alchemist who understands this has power over his life, as in achieving success, achieving peace and having a good, healthy life full of joy and abundance.

So welcome to chapter 14. If you understand the insights in

this chapter, you can create a beautiful life, you can create beauty and harmony, and you can create abundance, wealth and health in your life. It is the science of wealth. It is the science of becoming successful in any venture or journey, the science of gathering knowledge and insights, of finding celebration in your life, of achieving, reaching and ambition. This is the science which gives you insights in daily life and this is the chapter for nation builders.

Here we will discover why some societies became very successful and some failed. We will explore what made societies succeed in some fields, and what made them lose in other fields. Why some nations are more successful than others, why some nations master one thing, and other nations master other things. In this way, this science aids in understanding history.

When you understand it, it is a science, when you learn it, it is a knack, and when you master it, it is an art.

Swimming and driving is a knack. It is something you learn. Science you must understand. It is the pursuit and application of knowledge and understanding by following a systematic methodology based on evidence. So when you learn this, learn it like science. When you understand and practice it and start to know it, it is a knack that you will not forget. And when you master it, master it like an art. It is both an art, a knack and a science.

This is the **science of gunas** or the nature. Nature of what? Krishna says that nature is mother, and consciousness is the father, purusha and prakrti. Mother nature has gunas, which consciousness is aware of, which consciousness knows, feels and sees. The consciousness will feel, know and experience differently depending on which guna is present.

The gunas are **sattva, rajas and tamas**. These are the three important gunas, and mastering them is like an alchemy. When one guna increases, that particular nature starts to grow and manifest its qualities in your life.

What are the gunas? In the same way as the nature of fire is to burn, and the nature of the sun is to shine, the same is with the gunas of prakṛti. When you touch fire, you get burned. When light is there, you can see, and when the light is not there, you cannot see. The gunas each have a **different energy and frequency** which are there in the space, in the nature itself. They are in your body, in your daily life.

When someone says that there is a good vibe somewhere, it means their frequency is matching the frequency of that place, or that they like that frequency. Some may find a place very boring whereas others find it very peaceful, and some may find a place too intense whereas others find it stimulating and exciting.

There is a widespread misunderstanding that tamas is bad, rajas is less bad and one should only be in sattva. No, Krishna does not judge the goodness of the gunas. He just says gunas. And to be able to transcend, Krishna explains, you must go beyond all of them, including sattva. You must transcend all of them.

Now we will try to **understand the nature of the gunas**, and how they manifest in your life.

Let us start with the **guna of tamas**. Tamas is responsible for sleep. Without tamas, there is no sleep. Poor tamas got such a bad name. Krishna partly describes the nature of tamas in the Bhagavad Gita. At that time the unconscious tamas was at the peak, there was no sattva, and they were in the middle of battlefield, therefore Krishna is emphasising sattva. At that moment, in that context, Krishna is pointing out the consequences of unconscious tamas and rajas. Rajas has brought them all to battle. Krishna fought for sattva long before the battle. He went to everyone with the message of sattva, sattva, peace, peace, peace. But everyone was in tamas and rajas, and nobody listened to Krishna. Now he is repeating the emphasis on sattva. Understanding this context in which tamas, rajas and sattva is spoken about is very important. So the tamas nature got a bad reputation, but today we can correct it a bit.

Your sleep is predominantly due to tamas. Try not to sleep for three or four days, then you would know the value of tamas. But when tamas goes wrong, when conscious and love is lacking, it brings laziness, procrastination, carelessness, and an inertia which you cannot think outside. You are unable to get out of that inertia, whatever that inertia is. You find yourself in dead habits, dead routines, and dead ends of life. You can become very insensitive. And if there is no sattva, your life lacks vision.

With good understanding of tamas, with conscious tamas, you can have good rest and good sleep. You can **rest in the darkness of tamas**. You can develop good systems and a conscious inertia of good systems.

When we look at the history, who mastered tamas? Henry Ford mastered tamas. He developed new mass production methods, assembly lines in the factories, in order to manufacture his popular Ford car in sufficient quantities. This development demanded an understanding of each part of the manufacturing process, and it demanded creation of a system to support the efficiency of the process. This comes after this, and this comes after this. Keep repeating, keep repeating, keep repeating, keep repeating. With this mastery of tamas, the industrial powers built empires.

For 1000 years in India, there was an over-emphasis on

sattva, and rajas was looked down on. This resulted in India allowing invaders from the place where the unconscious tamas and rajas were at their peak. Not the conscious rajas which brings vision, ambition, progress and advancement of civilization, but the unconscious and unbalanced rajas and tamas. The invaders came and destroyed most of the major learning centres. Due to this understanding of the gunas, the alchemy of the gunas went wrong, and India, the spiritual powerhouse of the world, was put down by unconscious rajas and tamas.

See, all gunas can fall to the very low when consciousness and love are lacking. For tamas that means ignorance, carelessness, and uncontrolled and non-visionary inertia of habits and dead systems. Dead bureaucratic systems with files and papers moving without awareness, overview or vision. The movements are like a headless chicken, going round and round and round.

Tamas with love and consciousness brings preservation, taking care of the values, even taking care of the knowledge. For example, there were people who sat down and received the spiritual knowledge and did the task of writing and writing. Thousands of scrolls with spiritual knowledge and thousands of stupas were made, and in this way the knowledge was preserved–through the power of conscious tamas. Tamas also brings acceptance of how things are. It can bring endurance because the repetition is there. You are repeating the same thing, like walking uphill you keep taking one more step. This is a repetitive action, which is tamas. With the energy of tamas you can build good systems, like assembly lines and good bureaucratic systems.

Keeping **awareness of tamas** is essential in order to be able to notice if it starts going wrong or becoming unconscious. As Krishna points out, consciousness experiences, knows and feels the gunas. When consciousness feels procrastination or laziness, it means tamas has started to go wrong. When you end up in bad habits that spoil your health, like any kind of addictive habits, for example the dopamine addiction of video games or social media, know that tamas has started to wrong. Awareness of this comes from consciousness.

It is possible to convert bad habits to good habits and create good inertia of life. But how you will do that? Through rajas.

So, let us move on to **rajas**. Without rajas there is no advancement. You need aim, you need ambition, and you need a drive in your life. Without that drive, how can you reach anything? You need a burning desire, a burning passion to reach, to conquer, to inquire, to understand, to gather, to research, to vision and lead, to motivate yourself for whatever you are doing and to motivate others if you are with others. Without that motivation, that passion and that burning desire, you will not reach anywhere.

The burning desire of rajas backed by conscious tamas brings consistency and persistence. If you are learning music, get into at good consistent routine of practicing the same time every day. Challenge yourself to keep the intensity high. If you are in a learning process, and something takes you three hours now, challenge yourself to reduce the time to two hours and then to one hour. This is rajas. And sticking with your routine, doing it consistently every day and thereby creating a good inertia, this is tamas. Doing it right, learning the best music from the best teacher, reaching to excellence, this is sattva.

This is the alchemy of the gunas. Learning the alchemy of the gunas is key. By knowing it one can understand a lot about life. One must know which guna is which and understand how the gunas interact with each other. That is the science.

What is the energy of the gunas? What is the collective gunas of different places? How does it work? These are some core aspects to understand.

When there is **rajas with love and consciousness**, when it moves with full vitality, then it brings ambition, passion, enthusiasm, courage, and motivation. Rajas wants to advance things and move things into the right direction. Rajas wants change, innovation, and transformation. And rajas is persistent. Consistency comes from tamas, but persistency comes from rajas. Every day consistently doing what is needed, that inertia is from conscious tamas, but the persistency it takes to overcome whatever challenges arise on the way, rising up and continuing after failing, this comes from rajas. And the combination of persistence and consistency brings you success. Getting success in the right direction, not the wrong direction, this comes from sattva, from vision and overview.

If rajas lacks consciousness, restlessness comes. You feel overactive, jittery, like when you have too much coffee, even anxious. Attachment comes, attachment to actions, wanting to hold on to things, like material possesions, people, ideas or where you live. The unconscious rajas brings aggression. Rajas has started to go wrong due to lack of consciousness and love. Consciousness gives direction, and love gives the energy to move.

Do not try to escape from this unconscious rajas, but **see it and transform it**. Because the gunas is an alchemy, when they go wrong, it is like good wine changing into vinegar. You taste it, you know it. See the gunas as an alchemy. Master them like an art, practice them like an art, move into them like an art. When you feel irritated, frustrated or restless, know that there is rajas wanting transformation. Consciousness brings that transformation to rajas.

The gunas are in the prakrati, and they are just there. But what makes it fertile, what gives birth to it, is the consciousness. Consciousness is like a seed, and the guna is like the soil. So do not to be scared of the gunas. If you see procrastination, you know that there is tamas wanting transformation, and it means you can transform it.

It is an alchemy, and exactly how to **transform the guna** will be different depending on the person and the time. Sometimes you just need a sense of direction, sattva, and tamas or rajas will transform. Sometimes you need more rajas, and the tamas or sattva will transform. Sometime all you need is and understanding of the alchemy of gunas, and you will be able to see what is needed.

For example, you see that this moment is not doing things, now it is time for resting, and you transform tamas like that. Then tamas did not go into action. You see that now is not the right time to act as it is raining outside, you cannot do what you wanted to do, and there is not much inspiration either. Then put on some music and have a deep rest. Conserve your energy. Tamas is the best to conserve energy. Conserve your energy, and the right time will come. Look at the lions. They lie under the tree and enjoy tamas.

So, do not be scared of tamas, but do not use it as an excuse either. Just lying under the tree doing nothing all the time would be an excuse.

You need to know the alchemy of gunas. The insight of the alchemy comes from consciousness, purusha. **Purusha guides prakṛti**. Purusha transforms prakṛti. Consciousness, remember the word consciousness. Consciousness is attention, awareness, insightfulness, love, compassion, kindness. These are the dimensions of consciousness.

People view consciousness only as awareness, as someone

sitting in Buddha posture. No, Radha is also consciousness in her love and beauty. Radha, in her dance of love and beauty, is the same as Buddha sitting in awareness and peacefulness. This is **the feminine nature of consciousness**, do not dismiss it. We are no longer in the medieval times. India has always been respecting consciousness equally whether it expresses itself in form of love or in form of awareness.

Consciousness is that which will transform the gunas. When you are in love, rajas falls into harmony, tamas falls into harmony, but when you are just infatuated, the gunas go in the wrong direction. Love and awareness transforms the desire. The desire gets burned in the fire of rajas, and then the sattva transcends it. Rajas invokes the desire, and sattva transcends it into consciousness, into meditation.

This is what the art of tantra is about. This is the art of the tantric sciences. Kashmir Shaiv tantra, Vaishnav tantra, Bodh tantra. Some parts of tantra are exactly about the interaction of purusha and prakṛti. The science of the Vaishnav tantra explores how consciousness transcends or masters this alchemy of the gunas.

Krishna calls this, the alchemy of the gunas, **the greatest Leela** or play. Why? Because Krishna is able to move the gunas into whatever direction he wants at any time. This creates Leela in life. So, there is no need to shun the science of tantra. Understand how the gunas move, how consciousness interacts with the gunas, and in that interconnectedness tantra flowers.

The way to master the science, knack, and art of the alchemy of gunas goes through awareness, through love, through practice, through hard work, through seeing, and through diligence. Through this you will be able to master the alchemy of gunas.

Let us look more into the three gunas. As we discussed, when rajas goes wrong, it brings conflict, fear, anxiety and instability in your life. It brings aggression, violence, uncontrolled and blind desires. But **when rajas is in harmony**, it brings courage, vision, motivation, leadership, action, enthusiasm, responsibility and persistence. You feel spirited. Rajas takes you on hero journeys, on new adventures in life. You explore, go to new places and find new things. You start a new company, excited about entrepreneurship, wanting to reach success and make money. You want to be successful in life, you want to gather name, fame, wealth and health in your life. That is rajas in harmony.

So do not condemn rajas. It has a place. The societies which underplayed rajas were dissolved from the face of the earth. The Mayans were so focused on sattva, and they were completely destroyed by barbaric invaders. Those barbaric jackals did not even master rajas properly.

During the industrial revolution, tamas was mastered. The tamas energy organized things, built great assembly lines and good bureaucratic systems. But without vision and advancement, which is conscious sattva and rajas, tamas goes wrong. And **when tamas goes wrong**, it brings confusion, ignorance, carelessness and lack of motivation for advancement. You fell like you already know everything. Carelessness of the inner comes. There is no vision at all in your life. You are insensitive to what is happening in your life. You eat and drink whatever comes in front of you. You wake up at whatever time and sleep at whatever time. There is no control of your life. You are indifferent to everything, playing video games and spending hours on social media, destroying your life. You become a curse to yourself.

In the unconscious tamas, you are a curse to yourself, but with unconscious rajas you become a curse to others as well, and with **unconscious sattva** you can become a curse even to future generations. Unconscious sattva is one of the most dangerous phenomena. So learn the mastery of gunas, and stop the gunas going wrong at the level of tamas. If you reach to sattva without mastery of this alchemy, then even for generations to come, sattva can be destructive. For example, some thinkers put forward half finished thoughts, not properly thought through, without proper insight and not properly built, and some of their books became responsible for great violence on the human kind. That is sattva going wrong.

When sattva is there, reach to the peak of it, do not leave it half. Sattva guides your life, so have it properly.

Let us look more into **sattva**. What exactly is it? Sattva is the vision that comes from within, the vision which guides you. It comes in form of intuition, in form of intelligence, and in form of yearning for knowing, for learning and for improving you life. And when sattva transforms, when it starts to flower in its beauty, it becomes peace. It becomes harmony, everything falling into harmony. It brings clarity, it brings insights, and it brings wisdom.

But **if sattva lacks consciousness and harmony**, you hold on to ideas. It brings analysis-paralysis, indecisiveness. You know so much, but are unable to do anything. Too much analyzing and repetitive overthinking.

In sattva without consciousness, you are compliant to everything, saying yes without any rajas for saying no, and without tamas for bringing the inertia or consistency of the ability to say no. The Mughals come, you say yes, the British come, you say yes. The revolutionaries who say "no, we want freedom"—that is rajas. In the corrupted sattva, you become overly compliant and start saying yes to everything without the power of revolution inside you.

The corrupted sattva also brings self-righteousness and feeling of superiority. You think your ideas are the best, and you start to feel self-righteous. You know without question that your way is the right way to live. You start judging others, that they are just indulging in rajas and tamas while you are in sattva. That kind of self-righteousness comes. You start identifying yourself with the spiritual aspects of life more and start to look down on people who are not so-called spiritual.

Unconscious, unharmonious sattva can also bring avoidance of reality. You are unable to see things as they are and do not want to look into the reality of life as a whole. Escapism, lack of strength, commitment and endurance will be affecting your life and people around you.

Know that we cannot avoid reality. The reality will come to you, that is the reality. Rajas can attend that reality, so take refuge in conscious rajas and guide it with sattva. Sattva is a great guide. Sattva gives the overview, Rajas gives the drive, and tamas gives you the inertia of continuing in the same direction.

There is another way to perceive the gunas. One can see everything that goes wrong as tamas and everything going right as sattva, but that is not a proper way to perceive it because the gunas work together as an alchemy. It is an alchemy, it is a science, it is a knack, and it is an art. So understand and learn it is an alchemy.

Krishna points out that **a liberated being is one who transcends all the gunas**. Any attempt to hold on to sattva or rajas is futile. Do not stay limited to rajas without transforming your life, because when death knocks on your door, you will go empty handed.

I would like to emphasize that when Sattva goes right, nothing goes right like that. It brings compassion, selflessness, purity and spiritual growth in your life. It brings contentment. You feel fulfilled, you are peaceful. You have wisdom. When Rajas goes right, you are the hero who completes the journey. You go on adventures and you reach. When tamas goes right, you are the force with which everything moves. You have the sleep, that mother sleep, in which you rest, regenerate and become nurtured.

The mother's consciousness is tamas and sattva in harmony, with love and consciousness. An entrepreneur's success is conscious rajas and tamas in harmony. An entrepreneur who has not only been successful but has dedicated the success for the society, for uplifting humanity, this is a harmony of conscious sattva, rajas and tamas. So, lay the foundation of a nation on the principles of all the gunas.

In the West, **mastery of tamas** has taken place, but along with that, the focus has come on comfort, security, entertainment, pleasure and needs being fulfilled.

Comfort can easily turn into a comfort zone, where there are no new experiences or challenges, and there is no rajas to take you out from that. Then there are no hero journeys in your life. You no longer venture into new dimensions of your life, and the adventure of life goes missing. With too much focus on entertainment and pleasure, there will be no meaning in your life.

Do fulfill your needs, but not at the cost of meaning, not at the cost of your hero journey. Hero journey is conscious rajas, and meaning is conscious sattva. Do fulfil your needs, but not at the cost of good inertia or momentum which builds your life, and not at the cost of deep, restful sleep. If you become successful, but are unable to rest fully, then what success would that be? If you are unable to sleep properly, then what kind of success is that? If you have gathered much wealth, but your wealth is not serving the humanity, and there is no sattva in your wealth, then what is that wealth good for?

Each guna has its own energy, and when you travel to different places, you can feel the change in energy. A city has its own collective energy of sattva, rajas and tamas. Some cities mainly have the energy of tamas. When you enter there, you would know it, you would start to feel like that. There are cities in India with a wonderful sattva energy, and when you go to those cities, that sattva energy will affect you. When you go to other cities, the hero journey will start, the ambition will start. Bombay is a wonderful place for hero journeys. Many people full of rajas go there and achieve their ambition.

India is a destination of spirituality which means that India has put the guiding principle of sattva highest. Tibet has been a place for sattva. Nobody mastered sattva like Tibet. Nobody mastered sattva like India. At one point India also mastered rajas and tamas, and it has more recently started to go in that direction again.

Then there are societies which underplay sattva and mainly focus on survival and fulfilment of needs. Even when there is abundance and prosperity, they are still concerned with survival and fulfilment of needs. They are still limiting themselves to that. Their societies need spiritual advancement and advancement in art, culture, beauty and love. This is the advancement needed in those societies.

In the West many people suffer from loneliness, isolation and sadness. The reason for that is lack of sattva. Tamas is there. People live in good houses, have good beds and enough to eat, but there is no sattva, no guiding principle. Rajas is also lacking. There are no hero journeys, neither inner journeys of transformation nor outer journeys of success. There is habit and repetition, going to the same job, the same supermarket and coming back home, having a half sleep or something and then waking up, dependent on coffee for rajas. That is the sad story.

We must also understand how the **motivation of modern people** is being shaped.

Let us first look at the **fear of not surviving**, which is a frequent motivating factor in the life of people. For modern people, this is the fear that the ends will not meet. Many people live in that, just trying to make the ends meet, just making it from one month to the next, from paycheck to paycheck. This is lack of rajas, lack of entrepreneurship, lack of changing one's life. This is tamas taking over the life, and rajas going wrong with the fear, where the fear becomes the motivation. Instead, the motivation should be the hero journey, which is conscious rajas. The motivation should be mastering something, like getting into the inertia of learning a technique, learning music, or learning a new subject. The inertia of consistent learning, conscious tamas. That should define your life.

In modern times motivations like **fear of loneliness** often create **relations**. Relations should rise out of sattva. It should come from love, not from fear of loneliness, from unconscious tamas. Nor should it come from plain infatuation, like becoming infatuated with someone and ending up in a relationship. That is rajas gone wrong. Relations should come from a place of sattva. There should be a vision for the relationship. How do you vision your relationship? What kind of journey are you are going on together? Look at all the great romantic movies, where the couple is on a hero journey together, and they are exploring the intimacy. This is the dream. Rajas, the hero journey, building something together, creating something together, and then having that joy, that celebration of love. This is what the motivation of a relationship should be, not fear of loneliness, infatuation or some base desire.

Let us examine **what influences our goals** in today's world. It can be as simple as media or social media influencing the goals and values of people. For example, for many people, social media defines the ideal look and the ideal success one should have. Some of the most successful business people I have met were envious of Elon Musk's success, comparing themselves with him. Some very beautiful women think they are not beautiful, because they see all those Instagram filtered photos of women with thousands of followers. People compare their life with what is exhibited on social media and constantly feel depressed about their life.

These are the goals being set by social media. These are the social expectations. People expect you to be a certain way, that by a certain age you have achieved certain things.

Take control of your life. Do not let the motivations and goals of others define your life. Have your own motivations and your own goals. Invite sattva in your life with visioning. Build great relations and build a great life for yourself.

Much of the **struggle for modern people** stems from not understanding the three gunas. If you master the alchemy of the gunas, this struggle will disappear. What is this struggle? Let us look at **unconscious rajas.** For example you envy the success of your colleague, the new car he bought, and you want the same for yourself. You want to be in the same social group, so you have to have the same car or a bigger car. You are competing and comparing yourself with others continuously, and through that your motivations arise. That comparison and unhealthy competition is driving your life. Where is the vision from sattva guna? Where is the mastery of your rajas?

If sattva guides you, and you are motivated by conscious rajas, then you are a natural leader and can motivate yourself with the right passion for life. This is the way. Have a clearly defined vision, put your full intensity for advancement towards your vision, and build good habits to support the manifestation of your vision. Create the inertia of good habits in your life. Without inertia of good habits and without deep rest and restitution, you are not going anywhere.

This is the **alchemy for success**, this is alchemy for good luck. Krishna does not leave any room for doubt. He does not say that what happens is due to karma or luck. He provides the exact science for good luck and success. In the previous chapter he gave you the science of karma, here he is giving you science of luck.

Listen to Krishna, walk on the path of Krishna, he guides you to the best.

Whosoever is reading this, now is your time. Take control of your life, do not let anybody or anything define your life. This is your time.

Master the gunas and master your life. Become a leader of your life. Have a great vision and a meaningful life, bring the intensity, vitality and expansion of rajas into your life and selfless actions, build good habits, and have a peaceful rest at end of every day.

Chapter 15

Between Fleeting Shadows, a Light That Never Moves

In this chapter you will see **how to be free from the illusion of Maya**. How to be free from birth, rebirth and death.

First we must understand that when birth is there, then life and death are also there. Birth, life, death and the world in between are four pillars, and we will examine all of them. The string which is attached to all of them, what is that string?

Krishna explains how the tree of Maya keeps us in illusion, in this string, in this movement, in this circle of consciousness which goes from the world beyond birth to birth, life, death and the world after death. The same world going in circles. The tree of Maya Krishna calls it.

The tree of Maya is rooted in the three gunas, Krishna says, and the only way to cut it is through selfless devotion, which we looked into earlier. He also prescribes renunciation for this, but what is renunciation really?

Renunciation is usually understood as going away from your home and practicing meditation. If you are a monk or sannyasin that would be your path. I personally do not prescribe this path, but I do suggest taking time out from your daily life and devoting it to self-enquiry, devoting time to find your path in life, and devoting time to reflect upon your life. Take time away from your daily habits, from your so-called life. This time could be one month, two months, three months, a year, or even a few years. I definitely suggest such a periodical renunciation of the habitual life. Seeing the state of the modern world, where there is no time and attention left for self enquiry, it is of utmost importance to give time to yourself.

Whether you live in the world or whether you leave it to live in a monastery, meditate in a Himalayan cave or live as a sadhu, the mind may wander into Maya, the senses may crave pleasures, you may be running away from suffering, struggling with misery, or you may be busy in your routines for fulfilling the basic needs. So such renunciation means nothing.

But it is possible to live your life to the fullest in the world and yet be a renunciate. How is this possible? Because true renunciation is when you renounce identification with conditioned thought patterns, with the world of illusion, and with the body-mind. True renunciation is renunciation of identification with the future projections in form of the fruits of your karma, renunciation of identification with the burden of the past and the karmic impressions in form of memories and conditionings, and renunciation of the self in form of doer, karta and bhokta, in form of ego. When renouncing this, you will be able to live the present to the fullest, with full awareness, attention and sensitivity. And with this, the tree of Maya falls by itself.

The other way of cutting the tree of Maya is through devotion. Devotion is the easiest of all. Devotion is the foundation of all. Devotion is the core of all.

Krishna says that when neither such renunciation nor devotion takes place, then you will stay in the cycle of birth and rebirth, death and rebirth. But what is the **cycle of death and rebirth**? What is it that dies, and what is it that does not die? This you need to be able to see. Let us see how it works, step by step.

The sages have identified the different forms of consciousness we experience. They call the states jagrit, susupti, swapan and the last state turiya, which is beyond the three other states. Jagrit is when you are awake, susupti is when you are sleeping, swapan is neither awake nor sleeping, but in the dream state, and uriya is the state which is beyond.

When you dream, you are not aware that you are dreaming. Awareness of dreaming is very rare. One is sleeping. Do you see how quickly time just disappears when you sleep? You fall asleep and wake up after 8 hours. What happens during this time? Are you alive? If you ask the doctors, they would say you are fully alive. Your brain is functioning, you are breathing, and your heart is beating. But where are you? Can you define where you are? When you are awake, you are fully there. But in sleep, in the sleep state, what happens? One must see with awareness what exactly takes place when during sleep. Where is that I, you cherish so much? What happens to that I in the sleep? Your presence is still there. If someone calls your name, you will wake up. If there is a loud noise, you will wake up. If there is some kind of a threat, which is usually felt energetically, you will wake up. So there is a sense of awareness in the sleep.

Krishna says, this sense of awareness is a gentle sense of

jnana. It is an awareness or knowingness of falling asleep. The knowingness is how you wake up, when your name is being called during sleep. That sense of knowingness is there in the sleep.

When you dream you can see things, but how is that possible when your eyes are closed? Have you ever pondered on that? Your sensory impressions are there in your dream state. Your brain creates dreams from the memory. If you had to imagine and create your dreams, it would be very difficult, but the brain effortlessly conjures it up. You see faces, clothes, places, even very complex things which would be hard to imagine. Some people's dreams are very elaborate with colours, lots of feelings and sensations and a storyline as well. If you had to imagine this, you would find it very demanding. So how is it possible?

See, there is jnana and there are **sensory impressions**. It is not sensory perceptions, as the senses are connected to the body which is sleeping. But the sensory impressions are not connected to the body. The senses tend to dull with age, but the sensory impressions never dull. You still have the same sensory impressions in the old age, and the quality of the dream images is still the same.

The **karmic imprints** in the brain is a form of memory. Let us see how the karmic imprints happen in the present life. If you learn music, then initially the movements are very difficult, but with practice you can play the music even half asleep. Coming straight out of sleep you can play it. This is because of the impressions in your brain in form of conditioning. There is a second layer of that impression, a karmic impression of the action, which goes to the level of the spirit. In the same way as the sensory impressions form in the brain, the karmic impressions of the same phenomenon happen on the energetic level.

Some karmic impressions you are conscious of and some not. There are karmic impressions of the collective which you are unaware of, and on the spirit level or energetic level there are karmic impressions from which you can re-learn everything. Driving is a good example of this. If you know driving, then even after 20 years without driving, you would still be able to drive. The same with swimming. These are knacks that stay in the brain and go into the subconscious. Driving and swimming are phenomena on the level of body, but every decision you make and every action you take leave a karmic footprint, both in your own consciousness and in the collective consciousness, also called the interconnected consciousness or the streams of consciousness.

So now we have three phenomena: jnana, sensory impressions and karmic impressions. The fourth phenomenon is prana.

What is prana? There is a saying in India, "when someone dies, prana leaves the body". There is no saying that the soul leaves the body. The saying "Ātman left the body" came later with the Christian missionaries. Ātman does not go anywhere, Ātman is there. Prana leaves the body.

When the Westeners started translating Indian scriptures, they translated Ātman as soul. Ātman is not the soul as understood in the Western scriptures or biblical scriptures. No, that misunderstanding needs to be cleared once and for all. Ātman is Ātman, and Ātman does not go anywhere. The translation is not correct. You can translate it as a spirit, as an energy, but not as soul.

What do I mean by **energetic impressions**? Our energy is composed of different energetic movements or different expressions of energies. The prana energy is what gives us life. Prana is in lungs, heart, and brain. You receive it from air, food, and drink. That is why pranayama is associated with breath, and all yoga emphasises right diet. Prana is of utmost importance, and some things are considered to have more prana than others. The Ganga water is seen as pure and full of prana, and living in the forest, being in the caves, and standing under waterfalls is recommended in the ancient scriptures for increasing prana. Whatever you take in, whether food, water, or air, all is prana.

Prana is in constant movement. The sense of being or life, which originates from Ātman, becomes identified with the flow of prana called life. This prana, along with karmic imprints, forms your sense of self. It forms that one drop from the ocean of Ishvara. This prana stream becomes conscious, and it becomes **a stream of consciousness** as self. You are a stream of consciousness which is alive, moving, aware and conscious. This stream of consciousness has its own karmic impressions, and while living you form new karmic imprints. In this way, there is you - separate from all, from Ishvara. This you takes birth, dies and is born again.

This stream of consciousness which is you, how did it become you? It became you because it has sensory impressions from you, it has your karmic impressions, and it is your prana.

There are five different form of **vayu or streams** of which prana is only one. These days we call all of it prana, but in the past it was called vayu. There is prana vayu, apana vayu, samana vayu, udana vayu and vyana vayu. All the energy going into the body is prana, and all going out is apana. This movement is called prana-apana. The fire which creates the digestion and metabolism in the body is samana vayu. Then there is udana vayu, your expression, your speech. The upward movement of this vayu is udana. The interconnection of all these vayus is vyana, which is your nervous system, where all the memories are established in the body.

These vayu streams move **after death** in search of a new body. When it finds a new body, it roots itself there. The prana starts to develop the brain, the lungs and the heart. The apana starts to create the outward movement or flow of the body, like the kidneys and urinary system. Then comes samana, the movement inside the body, like the blood, the digestive system and the metabolic system. First this is directly connected with the mother, and the samana comes directly from mother. But in the next stage, samana starts to develop in the featus. The cells grow, and the featus starts to move, which means the udana and vyana systems have started to manifest in the body.

A sage is aware, and even after death the sage is aware. In the same way the sage is aware in sleep, awareness is there after death and in the rebirth. Maybe you also are such an advanced level soul that you are aware in the death and afterwards, but usually awareness is connected with the body. So most likely you will fall into a sleep-like state in death, and the process of prana-apana movement will happen automatically, according to your your karmic impressions, in the form of a stream of consciousness. Where you get born and how you are born, this usually happens automatically.

The core understanding in the **science of transcending death** is the importance of staying aware in the moment of death and afterwards. Keep the jnana, keep the awareness, keep the awareness, keep the awareness. It is about keeping the awareness so you have a choice when death comes. See awareness and devotion as a powerful boat in a vast river. This boat gives you the power to choose which shore you to land on, and it makes your journey smooth.

If you are unable to **keep awareness** with the body now, when the body is alive, then it is highly unlikely that you would be able to hold the awareness when the body dies. Krishna advices to give time to develop awareness, so you can master the art of dying. Develop awareness through inner renunciation of identification as well as periodical outer renunciation of your habitual life. This of utmost importance. If you do not master awareness now, forget about mastering it in the death. Most likely death will take over you. In the same way sleep takes over you in the night, death will definitely take over you, because the pain of leaving the body is very strong. You are going to fall unconscious, and in that unconsciousness there is no control of birth and rebirth. It all happens automatically.

Another important aspect in the process of transcending death is **mastery of prana and sensory perceptions**. Let us look at prana first. If you have learned the art of mastering your prana in different situations, then it is possible to move the stream of prana in the process of death and afterwards, in the process of birth.

Internal sensory perceptions point to pain and pleasure in body and mind, but this usually takes place without awareness. If you master these sensory perceptions through awareness and consciousness, then in the moment of death you will not be moved by the pain of the body or by the instant gratification of immediate rebirth.

Through **devotion and the path of jnana** you develop an **inner intuitive guide** that will aid you through the process of dying and the journey afterwards, showing you, "don't go to that birth, it is not a birth for you, but a birth in the animal realm or that is a birth in a different realm, do not go there". The inner guide will be your light. Start now. Let devotion and consciousness be your wings through life and beyond.

Krishna says, all of this happens in your consciousness. Consciousness is a vast phenomena. If you think your consciousness is limited to your body and brain, you are very mistaken.

When the body is there, that time is your opportunity for gaining mastery. Do not waste this opportunity, because **death is coming**, death is coming. Death is the only reality which you know. It is surely coming. You do not know anything about your life, but one thing you know about is death, and that is the one thing you always forget. That is the one thing you think will happen to others, not to you. It will happen to you. It is happening to you right now. You are not the same person as before. Right now there is death, every moment is dying, every day is dying. When the day is over, it is dead and the next day is born. This body is bound to die, but before that, gain mastery of your senses, gain mastery of your karma, gain mastery of your prana, gain mastery of your mind. Master it. Now is your opportunity, do not miss it. Take it, receive it. Understand this science, know this art, know this knack. Death is knocking on your door, and Krishna is giving you this great science. Receive it with open arms.

Krishna says, if you are aware of this divine knowledge now, if you master it now, you will master it in the death. For the one who masters it, there is a choice of when and where to take birth, because you can move prana. Otherwise you are at the mercy of randomness and your prarabdh karma, sanchit karma and agami karma. If you master your mind now, if you experience samadhi and living in the heart of devotion now, then in the death there is possibility of transcendence. Otherwise **your next birth** would be decided by your last dominant thought, your last dominant prana, your last dominant internal sensory experience, your last dominant energetic impression. It is quite random, and there is no choice.

You can test this with sleep. The last thought you have before falling asleep and the first thought you have in the morning are the same. Exactly the same is the case with death. So do not be at the mercy of chance. Do not gamble with your next birth.

If you are in a good place now, then you have a great opportunity, then you have a diamond in your hand. Do not waste your diamond by trading it with some silly karmic impression, some internal sensory experiences, some thoughts in the mind, or some ego. Do not trade it with that. Value this diamond and devote it in the service of the divine. Do not waste it. This life is a diamond, so cherish it and rejoice it. It is your diamond, it is your life. Devote this diamond for the divine. Devote this diamond for awareness.

Know liberation before you die. Learn awareness, learn devotion, and learn surrender. Learn to master your senses, learn to master your mind, and learn to master your karma.

This is your opportunity, do not waste it. This is your opportunity, do not waste it. Being one with divine is your right, claim it.

Find your inner strength through the path of **vid vidya ved vedant**. Vid or ability to know and see brings vidya or true knowledge which can bring ved or crystallisation of true knowledge and vedant or the peak of wisdom. Vidya, the inner insights, brings inner strength. Gain those insights, and through that develop inner strength. Take the path of vid vidya ved vedant, the path of insights, not the path of merely borrowed knowledge. This path is available to you, Krishna has introduced you it.

When you have this knowledge, when you know and master it, your path to Ishvara opens. Ishvara is the existential consciousness as God, as divine, as one, the one who is identified with the existential consciousness. This is your path to Ishvara, and through Ishvara, through devotion, you will reach to the Purushottama.

Chapter 16

Guided by Purity, Divine's Essence Begins to Show

In this and the following chapter you will get a good **basis for your spiritual journey**. To a certain degree these chapters are even more important than others, at least in the beginning of the spiritual journey. Especially today where people immediately jump into meditation techniques and pranayama. You can find very advanced techniques online, Instagram influencers teach meditation, and people with a short yoga course call themselves yogis and teach yoga. So, it is the general rule today that people start their spiritual journey without any basics.

First we will explore the inner qualities that Krishna indicates as essential for the seeker. The first quality is **fearlessness,** which Krishna highlights as one of the most important qualities. Be fearless. Develop courage. You will need that on the inner journey. You may think that the outer journey or the outer battlefield requires the most courage, but Arjuna needs more courage and fearlessness on the inner journey, as we see through the Gita. He is fearless, and that is why Krishna is there. The inner path is the path of the brave ones, the courageous ones. Develop this quality of fearlessness. Do not be moved by fear. Fear is a pity little force that makes ropes into snakes, that does not let you take decisions in life, and does not let you reach your full potential. Be fearless in your decisions, fearless in your thought. Do not be careless. Fearlessness is not carelessness. Especially young people confuse carelessness with fearlessness. Krishna is not saying be careless, he says be fearless. Many times he was accused of running away from battles. Krishna is the pinnacle of courage, but he does not indulge in stupidities. Know the courage and the humbleness which comes along with courage. Humbleness and courage, these are your best friends.

Straight after fearlessness, Krishna moves on to the quality of **inner purity**. What is meant by inner purity? Some people are pure hearted and innocent. Innocent is not the same as foolish, but sometimes they do go hand in hand. There is a book by Fyodor Dostoevsky, The Idiot, and the main character of that book is such a pure being, a pure soul. Have the purity of the innocence. Keep that innocence in you. It may seem like a good deal to be cunning and clever in the world, but remember that you are trading diamonds for stones. Do not loose your innocence in being street smart. You can be street smart but not at the cost of your innocence. Know street smartness, know the ways of the world, but never at the cost of your inner purity, your heart, and your innocence. Always protect your innocence, the childlike innocence in you, because that is your direct connection with the divine. If you lose that in the ups and downs of the worldly battles, then when you stand at the door to the divine, you may have a transactional or calculating mind, looking into your purse and calculating your money, or you may be attached to something petty and miss the great divine. All your cleverness and cunningness work up till death only. Innocence will go beyond death, but your cleverness and cunningness will not take you anywhere. Do not trade your innocence with anything. Your innocence is a jewel, protect it.

The devotees of Shiva are called Bhola, and Shiva himself is called Bhola, meaning innocent. Hanuman is a manifestation of Shiva, and he is the greatest devotee of Vishnu and the pinnacle of innocence. He is innocent like a child, yet he is very smart and knows how to move in the world.

Identify the innocence and purity in others also and protect it. Take care of the people who have this innocence. By taking care of it in others, you take care of it in yourself. You appreciate it in yourself by appreciating it in others, and by appreciating it in yourself, you appreciate it in the other. So take a good care of such people, it is very important.

Krishna then says, **take charge of yourself**, be proactive with your mind. If you decide that you want to meditate, before even a single thought comes, sit down in meditation posture. Take action straight away. Do not try to negotiate with your mind. Mind is very smart, and if you start negotiating with it, it will trick you. Change your behaviour, and your mind will change. The brave and hard working people in the armed forces know that mind is too complicated a fellow, so do not negotiate with it. Bring energy and quickness into your actions, when it comes to mastering yourself.

Another important quality is to **be upright.** Being upright is meant both figuratively as standing up for your values and being righteous and also literally as keeping your back straight and head high. Often this is confused with arrogance, but it is not arrogance at all. It is a sense of uprightness, of holding your inner and outer posture. There are communities in the world who, just by the qualities of fearlessness, inner purity, being quick in action and being upright, have kept greatness in their culture, in their spirituality and in their lives. The Sikh community is an example of this.

Krishna advices to develop these qualities. On these qualities, you can build.

Another point Krishna emphasises is to have **no hatred** towards others. Do not carry bad feelings for others. Do not carry grudges. By that you limit yourself, and the world view disappears from you. So do not let yourself be moved by something as tiny as a grudge. Be aware and learn from your experiences, but do not carry malice towards others. Learn and remember. Keep the remembrance. Forgive, but do not forget. Learn the lesson, but do not carry grudges, thereby limiting yourself to that person and losing the uprightness.

Tenderness of heart is indicated as another important quality. Have the courage to be vulnerable. Yes, you are independent, but when it is time to ask for help, ask for help. When it is time to show your wounds and pain, be vulnerable. Have the tenderness of a flower inside you. Do not be hard like a rock. Protect the tenderness.

Compassion is also identified as a crucial quality. In many ancient Indian traditions, like Zen, Jain and Tibetan Buddhism, the focus is on developing compassion. Why is compassion so important? Because, if you know yourself without developing compassion and purity of heart, you will not be developing the vital force which brings you to teaching, which brings you to the guru nature as this comes from compassion. I am not talking about people whose teaching is motivated by name, fame, money or power. No, the true guru is motivated by compassion and expression of the truth. And that has to build before enlightenment. Before enlightenment, before the full liberation, you must know this part of yourself. Before liberation, develop compassion through the service for others, through taking care of the humanity.

Be **humble**, Krishna says. Being humble means to know your limits. Do not think that you can do everything. Right now you are in a meditative space, and that is well and good, but remember the monkey mind. Have humbleness, and do not think that you are superhuman. If you develop bad habits, that will affect both your mind, your body and your energy negatively, and the people you spend time with also affect you. You are not immune. There is also an upper limit to the capacity of your mind, body and energy, so be humble. Know that you are in a body with certain limits. Your mind is a monkey mind, remember that. Do not expect the superhuman from your mind, body, energy or will. Know your limits. When you have this humility you will also have also compassion for others, and you will not be walking around as an arrogant asshole.

Have the quality of **patience**, because things take time. When you see the greatest successes, you do not know how many generations they have prepared for it in their family or how many lives that person has prepared for it. You have no idea, so have patience.

Have the persistence of rajas and the consistency of tamas in your effort. **Consistency, persistence and patience**, these are some of the essential qualities Krishna describes.

From the beginning of your life, develop a habit of **giving and supporting others**. Give to charity, because with that you have a greater purpose for your work. Volunteer or give money for causes. Learn to give. If you are not even able to give money, then how would you be able to devote and surrender to divine? If you have never given time or money, but only traded your work in exchange for payment and fruits of the action, then this attitude of stinginess would reach to love.

No matter how poverty stricken you are, you still have half a chapati to give. Even if you are sleeping hungry, you still have one bite to give to the dog who is even more hungry than you or to the little monkey who is sitting and looking at your chapati. So, **learn to give**. Giving is easier when you do not have, because then you know the pain of not having. When you have, you are far from the pain, up in your castle eating cakes. At that time, you need to come down and see what others are going through. Learn to give, it is a key quality.

Have the quality of **truthfulness or authenticity.** Do not limit truthfulness to the spoken word, it is a much bigger phenomenon. It is about honesty with yourself and others, not being a hypocrite but authentic to your inner being, not pretending to be what you are not. Let the inner space of truth express itself in your life. Let your clothes reflect it, let your words reflect it, let your personality reflect it and let your actions reflect it.

Do not let **emotions** overpower you, whether it is the emotion of fear, anger, greed, desire, hopelessness or any other kind of emotion. Do not let it overpower you. Know and understand these emotions. When you look at it, when you shed the light of attention and awareness on to these emotions, you would know that they are ropes, not snakes. Know it, see it. See the power of awareness. In the West the stoics have worked on it, and in the East the Sāṃkhya school and Jiddu Krishnamurthy have done good work on this, opening up each emotion.

What is fear? Are you projecting fearful scenarios into the future? Is it a thought which is creating fear? Is it your ego causing fear? Open the emotion and look into it. Do not suppress it or hide from it, because then you put it in the underground world of shadows. If you push fear into the shadow realm instead of dealing with it, then at the moment of death you would be the biggest coward, the most scared person. Do not let that happen, attend the emotions properly.

Be **nonjudgemental**. Some people judge others in the name of spirituality or being so-called close to Krishna, thinking themselves superior. Do not look at others in contempt, especially with your friends and loved ones, do not look down on them. You have no idea about the circumstances of the other person, so do not carry that hypocritical superiority. Be a truly higher human being by cherishing and mastering the core values that take you to transcendence.

Krishna emphasises **yajña,** saying, do every moment as yajña. He calls himself Adiyajña. I am the yajña of the all yajñas. Giving your breath to Krishna, giving every moment to Krishna, devoting everything to Krishna, this is yajña. Devote yourself to love, to truth, to the inner self, to Ātman. Be that devotee, be that pinnacle of devotion. And through that devotion perform yajña. In every action, in every breath, in every moment be that. Be yajña in yourself.

Krishna points out **non-violence** as an essential quality. Krishna and Arjuna are in the middle of the battlefield and Krishna is emphasising non-violence. That seems odd. Before the battle Krishna was the one who stood most for peace. From the very beginning, he said no to war. Without knowledge of the background, Krishna may appear as a war monger, but that is completely wrong. Krishna is the pinnacle of peace. The war has arrived, and now Krishna is not shying away from the battle. He is not letting the Kauravas trample the good people. He is standing up for goodness, protecting the goodness in the world, and he clearly shows what he means by goodness by pointing to the qualities in this chapter.

Krishna also emphasise the **ability to feel deeply**. Feeling is a deeper phenomenon. Love happens in everybody's life at certain time, but some people are able to feel it deeply. Compassion takes place in everyone's life, but some people are able to feel it deeply. They have that tenderness, that sensitivity, that courage and that patience required to feel deeply. So develop these qualities needed to feel deeply, and develop a habit of feeling instead of straightaway reaching to conclusions, like an artificial intelligence identifying that "this is greed, and this is joy". Yes, all that is great, but did you feel it? Did you feel the beauty of the flower when you looked at it? Did you pay attention to that? When you walk into your room, do you pay attention to the interiors? How do you feel in that room? How does the chair you are sitting on make you feel? How does the person you are meeting make you feel? Pay attention to the feelings that arise.

The feelings do not lie, so be aware of them. Emotions lie all the time, so develop the ability to differentiate between feelings and emotions. Through that you would know intuition, and through that you would reach good insights.

Feeling deeply It is a very feminine phenomenon. Women have this practical intelligence, which is slowly becoming arcane, a lost art, as our cities do not support it. But the feelings have been guidance of women, which has stopped wars and other catastrophes. And if the people in power had listened to the advice from women, based on this intuitive emotional intelligence, then the world could have been a better place.

Develop **sincerity and authenticity**. Courage, sincerity and authenticity, with this, anything can be achieved. These are your best friends. Be sincere, be brave, be courageous, and be authentic. This is the heart of Krishna's message.

Develop **goodness**. When goodness is there, express it and assert it, because when goodness is not asserted, the ego definitely asserts itself. The greatest harm in the world happens when goodness is not asserted. Do not let the bad assert itself at the cost of goodness. Goodness needs to go out there, speak, act, and do what is necessary, do the right thing, do the righteous thing, do the duty in form of dharma. This is goodness.

When love does its duty, when compassion acts, when goodness leads, and when the purity of heart celebrates and defines art, culture and beauty, then the world becomes a better place. When authentic and sincere people master technology, advancement of the civilisation happens. When people with clarity of heart hold power, and the wealth comes to the compassionate, then this world becomes a better place, a beautiful place.

Then Krishna moves on to identify the **characteristics that take you away from divine**. These traits you must identify in yourself. Do not think yourself as an all great human being with no bad qualities. This knowledge is for you to find out in yourself, not to start pointing it out in others. Be aware of it in others as this helps you to be aware of it in yourself, and when you are aware of it in yourself you will be aware of it in others.

One of the biggest of these traits is **ego**. Having self-respect, self-esteem and standing upright is not ego. Ego is about 'me' and 'my'. It can be a 'poor me' or a 'great me' or some other type of 'me'. Some people make it about 'us and them', but it is still ego, just a little bigger circle where the leash for the dog is a little longer. These are egos which leads to battle, like us and them, "we are right, and they are wrong". Really? Have you looked into a mirror? Have you really enquired into it?

Do not divide the world in such a simplistic way. **We are all interconnected**. Everything is interconnected. Try holding your breath for two minutes, and you would know the value of the trees producing oxygen, you would know the value of nature. Try not eating for five days, then you would know the value of the farmer that produces your food. Know the value of the people protecting your borders. See how your house is constructed, your drainage systems. You are not the centre of the world. There is a whole world around you. Just bringing your cup of coffee to your table requires thousands of people. Have respect for that. Through this book you are learning this great ancient knowledge. How many people have kept this knowledge, protected and preserved it for you to have it right now? Knowing and valuing this interconnectedness brings humbleness.

Ego is a very complex phenomenon which cannot be simplified, but it is definitely that which takes you away from interconnectedness, oneness and divine.

Men and women often experience ego differently. Men tend to experience ego more as "I" and "me", whereas women tend to experience ego more as "my", like my relations, my man, my son, my house, my body. Such obsession women have with their body. My body, my eyes, maybe I change this, maybe I change that. This obsession of "my" is quite big in the ego of women. The same is with "me" and "I" for a man. I think that, I want that, I am right and you are wrong. This is what led to the battle at Kurukṣetra. Duryodhana was not letting a single piece of land go, so stuck with "me" and "my". I am superior, I should be the king, look at me, I am the great Duryodhana with all these great kings supporting me, Bhishma and Drona at my back, look at me. That "me" led to the battle.

Krishna points out **arrogance** as another trait to be aware of. Thinking yourself as the most important person, and that you know the right way and therefore not listening and not understanding. We see it in the court of Dhritarashtra. Everybody there is feeling superior in knowledge. They were all sure, they knew what was right. Do not let that arrogance take over you, thinking yourself more important or higher because you have knowledge, wealth, name or fame. Or maybe you have nothing but a constantly complaining poor-me-self, feeling self-righteous in your misery and complaints about your circumstances, thinking your own story of victimhood very important. The arrogance also show itself when someone actively tries to diminish others in order for themself to be higher. By doing that you cause harm to yourself, and you destroy your soul. Because you are a coward, you want to hold superiority and look down on others. Do not do that.

Cowardice and weakness of values are two other traits to look out for. Dhritarashtra keeps referring to "my son, my son". He is struggling with cowardice and weakness of values. He does not know his values, what he stands for, and he is letting his son decide everything and eventually becoming the cause of death of so many people. The story of Jesus and Judas is similar. Judas was a coward with weak values, and Jesus suffered from that. The combination of weak values and cowardice is dangerous, both to yourself and to people around you, because with cowardice, fear can easily grip you, and if you are not backed by strong values and principles, then others can easily influence you and make you take bad decisions in that state of fear. So know your values, build strength in them, and stand by them. If your values are love and beauty, guard and protect those with your life. If your values are love, compassion and courage, stand by and protect those values. And protect the people who carry those values.

Krishna warns not to let your **emotions cloud your awareness**. Neither fear, anxiety, greed or desire should blind you. Do not end up living a slave life because you want to live in a certain house, and you want to drive a certain car. Do not let blind desires define and guide your life. Do not let greed guide you, accumulating what you do not need. Greed can be of things, of spiritual experiences, of power or popularity, like followers on Instagram. Krishna warns not to let those emotions blind you and define your life.

Krisna then points out **untruthfulness** as a trait to be aware of in yourself. Some people are fearful inside, but outside they wear a **mask of power and control**. All their time is about keeping the control. They want to control how you think, and who you are. Be aware of this tendency, both in others in yourself, that whenever the fear strikes, you want to control. That tendency to want to control and manipulate people, be aware of that in yourself. Do not let that guide your life. Do not move others with that. Whenever you see yourself going that direction, be watchful. It is rooted in fear. You are a coward rooted in your cowardice. Do not be that coward wearing a mask of strength whose whole life is about control and power. Do not walk that path, it leads to hell.

Then Krishna makes us aware of **violence** as another trait or tendency to avoid. Violence can be of many kinds, like hurting physically or hurting the feelings, putting the other down and destroying their inner space or the space they have in the minds and hearts of other people, either by gossiping, by backstabbing or worse. Some people find pleasure in deliberately harming and hurting others. The Machiavellian mindset of controlling others while hiding securely behind masks is an example of this. They present a polished face of friendliness and good intentions, while the inside is busy scheming for your downfall, thinking ten steps ahead. Be aware that everything that glitters is not gold, and everything that looks holy is not holy. Do not walk that path of hurting the other. In the longer run you will hurt yourself, and the damage you cause to your soul cannot heal.

Krishna also says, be aware of traits like **lack of emotion and feeling**, like in sociopathy. The intellectual understanding of the emotion is fully there, but there is no feeling, no empathy towards the other, and there is carelessness of the action and whether it hurts others and an arrogant attitude of 'me-me-me'.

Develop **sensitivity** towards nature, towards people and towards life. Without that sensitivity you would not be able to identify Krishna if you met him. So many people missed him in his own time. It is Arjuna, who is pure at heart, brave, and courageous, who sees Krishna. It is Radha, who is in love with beauty and compassion, who sees Krishna.

If Krishna came to your life, you would miss, because you would be looking for him on the stage, wearing a glittering mask of holy clothes, a spiritual look and a smiling face. You would not see, that the person playing flute and taking care of cows is Krishna. You would totally ignore him because you are waiting for a great sage to come down from the mountains. So be aware, the great people are not necessarily those with great names.

Today everybody revers the great Lord Krishna and the holy Bhagavad Gita, but in his own time, how many people went to Krishna to learn? Arjuna did, because Arjuna is special. He is pure at heart. He is brave. He is visionary. He is honest. All his questions are honest. He is questioning, he is doubting, he is authentic. That is what reaches to Krishna.

Look at Radha. Radha is in love with beauty. Radha is in love with love. Radha is in love with devotion. Radha is in love with compassion. Radha is in love with art, with the nature, with prakṛti. That is what is required. These qualities bring her to Krishna. She is not seeking for a great teacher to descend from the stage. You would miss. You would totally miss. The mask is not the real thing. You can have a great brand and great appearance, but that has nothing to do with truth.

Krishna warns with utmost clarity not to be moved by the traits which take you away from divine, neither inside yourself nor in people governed by them. Sometimes these forces work through the collective, and as most people are governed by the collective, they tend go along with it without much questioning. No, have **individuality**. If you do not develop individuality, your own thinking, your own feeling, ability to have your own judgment, then you will be easily influenced by the collective. If you are moved by the collective, you will not stand when the evil forces are walking on the goodness. You will not able to stand, and most likely you will not even able to even identify it because it happens so slowly. When the temperature rises in the pot, the frogs do not notice it before it is too hot and the death comes. So develop individuality, critical thinking, judgment, intuition and feelings. More than critical thinking feeling is important. So be aware when you are moved by the herd. You would need your individuality, your clarity of thinking, your clarity of feeling, your clarity of insight.

Develop individuality now, at this moment, whatever stage you are in life. Read the great philosophers and thinkers. Study psychology. Immerse yourself in art and culture. Culture has developed over millennia as a crystallised learning, and art and culture give you the roots and space for you to ignite and grow individual intelligence.

And if you do not read, then **develop intuition, develop feeling**, develop the feminine power. Develop selfless action and experiential learning. Connect deeply with diverse people from different backgrounds, that is experiential learning. Learn by meeting and connecting, learn by serving. When you serve people, when you meet diverse people every day, you would get to know a lot about people, and by that, you would know a lot about yourself.

Know, understand and develop an intuitive feeling by connecting with nature. Nature will guide you. How did the hermits who live in nature become so wise? Just by being in nature. Nature has its own intelligence, its own collective. So go away into nature. Go hiking, go trekking, go into the mountains, go into the forest, sit with the rivers, stand under waterfalls and sit next to fire.

Learn **periodical renunciation** of your habitual life. Take time out, not just in organized retreats. Take time out for yourself so that you can reflect upon things. These days this is even more important because the power of the herd is in your pocket. You watch videos on social media, and you do not notice how the narration in your mind changes. So take charge of your narration, that is crucial.

Take responsibility for yourself. Be accountable for your own emotions, thoughts, values, actions and meaning. It is easy to not accept the responsibility for yourself and leave the responsibility of your emotions, thoughts and actions and to others. Instead of attending difficult emotions and thoughts, enquiring into them and facing them, you choose to perceive somebody else as the cause of your state. This is bound to create drama in your own and others' lives through blaming, crying and feeling like a victim of life.

Have **deep roots in meaning** and develop **life affirmative values**. If you are unable to find meaning in life and do not have deep rooted values, you are bound to break in the difficult times. Without the strength of values the difficult times will break you. There is a beautiful book on this by Viktor Frankl, Man's Search for Meaning. Frankl was a psychiatrist who was put in a concentration camp by the Nazis. There he experienced how only those people who were able to give strong meaning to life and root themselves in values of life survived the horrible circumstances.

You have a long way to go. You have a great path ahead of you. So be the force of goodness, be the force of truth, be the force of love, be the force of courage, be the force of compassion, be the force of purity of heart. Be sincere, be authentic, be who you are. Know that with these values you can walk on the path of Ātman. If you think that Ātman or Krishna will come to your life without you mastering these values, forget about it. This is your path to Krishna. It is a demanding path, but with love for Krishna, it is effortless, like Ganga in search of the ocean. It looks like such a long journey, but Ganga is dancing and celebrating and reaching the ocean joyously.

I emphasise **celebration and humour**. Learn to laugh, have the intelligence which laughter brings. Good, intelligent laughter, intelligent compassionate humour and a life of joyous celebration of devotion.

Remember that the guidelines in this and the following chapter are the basis of the spiritual journey, they are not meant as an easy way around sadhana and practice. The real thing is self inquiry, selfless action, devoting your every breath, every thought, every feeling, and every moment to Krishna. That is the real deal. Sometimes people see these guidelines as an escape route. They start following these guidelines and then look down on others, without even doing what Krishna is asking, which is abhyas or practice, meditation, self inquiry, selfless action and great devotion.

Chapter 17

In Tamas, Rajas and Sattva, Life's Tales are Told

The three gunas, tamas, rajas, and sattva, affect the life in many ways that people are rarely aware of. In this chapter Krishna explains how the different gunas affect our connection with the divine, connection with food and the way we give or share with others.

Unconscious tamas mainly shows as ignorance, laziness, carelessness, and the inaction which comes from that. That type of inaction is not the same as the inaction arising from meditation, peace or silence, which is a great action. Unconscious tamas **affects our connection with the divine** by bringing ignorance, laziness and carelessness to how we relate with the mystical or divine aspect of the existence.

One form of ignorance is just living according to whatever conditionings and ideas we got during our upbringing, without questioning it in any way, and without even looking into the matter. If you grew up with the idea that there is no

God, and everything is about science, money, labor, and the material, then that is your relation with spirituality.

Another form of ignorance is blind belief, for example blindly believing in stories which makes no sense or in stupid ideas. Krishna points out that blind belief is tamas. Any kind of blind faith without inner enquiry is tamas. The inner enquiry does not have to be only a scientific inquiry, because you can see and know with other abilities than logic, like feeling or intuition, as the Vedas point out. When working with logic have clarity and purity of reasoning, because logic has fallacies which limit the reasoning.

Ignorance can also be of habitual limited thinking. You do not even think about divine. Krishna clearly points out that this is ignorance.

Krishna does not ask you to blindly believe him. See for yourself. Do the practices, meditate, live selfless action, and live a life where love reaches the depth of devotion. How does it feel when love has courage, trust, surrender, devotion, compassion, empathy and sensitivity? What does love for divine mean? See for yourself. Does it bring joy and celebration in your life? Krishna's message is, that you must see it and know for yourself.

You may be meditating for good sleep or doing asanas for good health or similar ambitions. You may go to the temple to ask for material success in your life. You may have some idea of enlightenment and the goal of reaching that becomes your ambition. All this Krishna defines as properties of rajas. Be aware that this is **rajas driven worship**. Do not judge it though. The one who is ignorant today could tomorrow be highly devoted to life and divine. Someone who is now stuck in blind faith could tomorrow be a wise enlightened being. You never know. So do not judge rajas as higher or lower, just see it as it is. Rajas brings ambition to the worship. Ambition for enlightenment and connecting to divine for achieving material success and power. You can obtain many different siddhis from your meditation, and you can ask for great success in life. That is rajas showing itself in the connection with the divine.

Krishna says that the best is when there is a **sattva or clarity in the connection with the divine**. You are on the path and have done the hard work of practice and self-enquiry, wisdom comes, and you are intuitively aware of the transformation happening. With this comes clarity, compassion and selflessness, the devotion flowers, and you worship for the sake of worship, for the sake of being in love. That is the greatest worship, Krishna says.

When someone offers a simple flower, or even a leaf, in full of devotion, then that devotion reaches to Krishna. It is far better to be in that state of devotion without knowing any mantras or rituals than it is knowing the mantras and rituals without the devotion, as it is the devotion that reaches.

Krishna says, a selfless action which is not motivated by attachment to the results of the action, which is not burdened by duty without joy, and which is motivated by love for your dharma, for your action, for devoting that action in the service of the divine, this worship reaches to Krishna. This worship is directly connecting with the divine aspect of Krishna, with the divine aspect of this existence, with the Ishvara principle. So your selfless action reaches to Ishvara principle.

If your heart is totally surrendered and devoted in love, then an offering of a simple flower as a worship reaches divine more profoundly than hundred days of rituals, chanting, yagyas, asanas and pranayamas. If you are you devoting your breath to the divine, to the Ishvara principle, that reaches profoundly.

Krishna warns against the blind following of tamas. Do not go into that. And be aware of rajas in your worship or practice, if it is merely for gaining something rather than selfless action. Do not see it as bad though, as it is a journey. Sometimes there are a difficulties in life and you pray in distress. That is perfectly fine. Or you do meditation for good sleep. Better do it for good sleep than not doing it, but it is important to be aware of.

Aim for sattva in your connection with divine, aim for clarity and purity in your heart. That purity will radiate into whatever you do. It will spread itself into your devotion, into your action, into your self-inquiry, into your abhyas and into your meditation. So bring your worship, your faith, your devotion to this clarity, purity, wisdom, and compassion. Focus on the depth of the feeling, focus on the depth of sincerity. These principles of sincerity, depth of feeling, trust and surrender are the principles that will guide you. That is Krishna's message.

Do not stay in ignorant tamas. Enquire, travel and see the world, open yourself to different ideas. Do not live in a closed dimension. Do not fall victim to blind craziness or extremism. Do not ignore the important questions of life and just continue in carelessness. Do not fall into that, be aware.

Welcome the passion and ambition of rajas in your life. It is fine to meditate for deeper sleep and increased mental capacities. There are many meditation apps to help you with this. Just do not let it define the devotion as it is not pure devotion. The purest devotion is with full sincerity, trust and compassion. Aim for that, and let that be your expression. And when you see it in others, when you see someone with purity of heart and innocence, who is in total devotion, then support and take care of them. That is important. Protect those values.

Now Krishna's focus moves to food. **Food is about prana**. It is the way you connect to nature, because prakriti is the core aspect of the food and prakriti is full of prana. Different pranas are in prakriti, and every food affects the prana and the gunas in you. Guna and prana are the key aspects of the food.

First it is important to develop sensitivity to your body's response to food, to develop **awareness of your body's signals**. Your body has developed over billions of years and it has its own intelligence. Listen to your body, it has messages to give. When it is tired it tells you that it is sleepy or when it is hungry it will make you aware of it. When the body gets proper sleep and you wake up without need of an alarm, that intelligence is in the body. The body tells you that now it is time for food. So first develop this sensitivity in the body.

Today we live in box shaped houses, totally disconnected from the nature, totally disconnected from the **rhythm of the nature**. When you spend time in nature you start to connect with the rhythm of the nature. When you go and live in the forest for some time, climb mountains, go for hiking or trekking your body adapts to rhythm of the nature. You will wake up early morning. You cannot stay sleeping in the tent after sunrise, it is just not possible. When you connect with the nature, the body aligns with the rhythm of nature, so learn the rhythm of the nature.

Next connect to the prana in yourself know through **pranayama**. Many diet issues can be corrected through yoga asanas and pranayama. When you practice yoga asanas and pranayama, you become aware of the prana in your body, and you will start to notice how different types of food affects your prana. When people with problems of addiction or bad food habits start doing asanas and pranayama regularly, the craving for drinking or overeating often disappear. In this way, eating rightly by giving the body what it needs without stuffing it, this often gets corrected by itself. The reason is that the sensitivity of the body increases, and the awareness or sensitivity towards prana increases so you feel the prana of what you are taking in. You start to become aware of different forms of prana or vayus, and with that awareness you become aware of the prana of the food, of the nature, and of other people's prana.

Another aspect of connecting with food is the **process of cooking**. When a mother, devoted to motherhood, cooks food in love for the children, the food carries that prana. Some of the people fighting in world war one and two wrote in their diaries how they missed the food of their mother or of their beloved. This is what they were missing. The prana, the love you share and put in the food. Food is not just an empty medium, some molecules and nutrients as describes on the back of the package. Food is prana. How you grow the food, how you cook it, how you bring the food from the farm to the table, and what relation you establish with the food in the process, all this goes into the food. The same words can turn into poetry or into a scientific inquiry, and you can say the same thing in a different tone, and it would get a totally different meaning. The same is the case with food. Food carries not only prana, it carries love. It is very important to know when cooking and serving food.

The highest of the high is when you devote food or prepare food for the divine, for Krishna, when you prepare and serve food for the Ishvara consciousness. Before you eat, serve food for the divine.

When you prepare something, for example a cup of chai, be very aware of the quality of the ingredients, like the origin of the milk, the spices you add, the kind of sugar you use. The quality really matters. The quality of the ingredients and the quality of the process of preparation, that is at the heart of the food.

If you decide to live on a very specific diet, like not eating onion and garlic, or only eating apples, or only drinking juice, and you then view everybody who eats or drinks differently as some lowly creatures, then you are hurting your soul. Do not think that you know what is right. If you look down on people because of their food habits or how they worship or connect with the divine, you hurt your soul, you hurt yourself. It is not good for you in your spiritual growth or in your life, so pay attention if any such judgments come. Be aware that you are not looking down on anybody. You do not know the situation of the other, how their life is, what kind of background they come from, so do not put any judgments on other people.

Krishna now moves on to talk about **the gunas in food**. Every food has its own guna. Freshly cooked food, rightly farmed food is more rich in prana. Good vegetarian food carries a lot of prana, and it gives more prana than it takes in the process of digestion.

So be aware of the diet. There is no diet prescription for everyone at all times in life in all situations. You have to develop sensitivity to the needs of your body.

Some foods bring passion, some foods bring ambition, that is more like energy. For example coffee brings a lot of rajasic energy. You need that rajasic energy to be able to do big things, to be able to reach. It was not a coincidence that the great stock markets and great companies were started in coffee houses, from Amsterdam to New York. But be aware that the rajasic energy may come in the way of deep rest or self-enquiry. Being aware what the food does to your body is the key.

Different food is suitable for different circumstances. Survival food is good if you live in a forest or in the mountains, if you are a hunter-gatherer or in times of war.

Be aware how different foods increase different elements in you. If you eat heavy food, not rich in taste, not properly cooked, old food or food just cooked for profiteering without any passion or care, like in a dirty and careless restaurant, not only can you fall sick from that food, but it will also take more prana than it gives, and it will affect your thoughts and your emotions negatively.

People who start doing yoga and pranayama regularly often experience their food habits changing for the better, and with improved food habits their life improves. They have more energy, more time available, better sleep, better mental and emotional health, less issues, and are more successful in their life.

If you struggle with issues like bad food habits, dependency on alcohol, dependency on easy dopamine from video games or social media or a highly stressful life, start studying Bhagavad Gita and doing pranayama. I know that if you practice yoga and pranayama and read Bhagavad Gita every day, your life would change. I stand by this. Take care of your life. Start with five minutes practice of pranayama every day and then slowly increase it, first to ten minutes, then to half an hour. Learn a meditation technique and do it three times a week, increase it to five times a week, increase it to seven days a week, and then make it one hour a day, then give it one hour in the morning, one hour in the evening. Do asanas, do pranayama, and in one year you would be a transformed human being as the sensitivity of your body would grow.

Now we come to a very important part that can be life changing. For me this has been the most essential part of life. That is **giving, sharing**. If you master this, a multi-dimensional expansion is possible in your life. With the insight Krishna gives here, you can totally transform your life, and the prarabdha karma, meaning the coming hurdles, can be removed. Your sanchit karma that gets activated and becomes prarabdha can be removed. And dhrid adhrid karma, which is stubborn karma that is just there and is very difficult to remove, that kind of karma can also be removed with this. So with this, you are no longer just at the mercy of your karmic imprints.

What is giving? What is sharing? Let us look into it.

See, Krishna could have chosen not to participate and stayed in Vrindavan instead of helping the Pandavas, but Krishna did participate. He volunteered, he acted, and because he stood for the truth, for the dharma, today we have Bhagavad Gita. Krishna could have decided not to share this knowledge with Arjuna, but fortunately for us he decided to share. Buddha could have decided to stay in silence, but instead he decided to speak.

Giving or sharing is the defining factor between great, mediocre or lowly, because with sharing, suddenly everything is different. Imagine if the artists of the great artworks had not shared their art, or they had chosen to do only the art they were paid for, only because of the money, not because of the passion, not for expression of creativity. This world would be filled with mediocrity.

Steve Jobs was not motivated by designing computers. He was motivated by taking the humanity forward through technology. That motivation brings a totally different expression. He volunteered for taking the humanity forward. He gave his body, mind, heart, work, action, money, property, everything he gave for the cause of taking the humanity forward. This also gave him great wealth, name and fame.

Warren Buffet could have chosen not to give his wealth and just kept it all to himself, but he donated a big part of it to charity. And a lot of innovation has come from it, a lot of education and a lot of hospitals. Some of the greatest institutions in India are built by Tata Trust. From those institutions great scientists have come, great innovators have come.

Your karma changes when you give. Your prarabdha karma, your dhrid prarabdha karma, which is the most difficult to change, even that can be changed with giving. The society karma can also be changed with giving, that is how big scale effect giving has.

The art of giving, the art of sharing, the art of expressing, that is what Krishna is pointing to here. If Krishna had decided not to give, what would have happened? So many liberated beings Bhagavad Gita alone is responsible for. Imagine if that day Krishna had said, no expression, but he is letting the truth express itself through him for Arjuna to receive. This is the highest form of giving which Krishna is showing by action.

These days money is one of the dearest phenomena for people. If you are unable to give, start with giving money, which is the most difficult, then give or volunteer your time and dedicated energy. Give just for the sake of giving. That is the art of transforming your karmas through gratitude and giving.

Krishna points out **how the gunas affect the giving**. Tamas shows itself in giving and sharing when the giving is driven by ignorance. For example, in Mahabharata, Karana was a wonderful person, a great warrior and a very giving person who ended up supporting Duryodhana against Krishna's advice. Still he was held very high in Krishna's eyes for his nature of courage and gratitude. Another example of tamas-driven giving, is when the giving makes you feel superior. Still, tamas-driven giving it is better than not giving, because by giving at least you change your own karma.

Now, better than that is the ambition- or passion-based giving, the **rajas-driven giving**. You are passionate about a cause and donate to it, but you want your name highlighted as a donor, or you want an experience in return, or you want to get close to the person to whom you are giving, or you want to reach to the front line of your guru, or you want to make the greatest, highest and biggest temple. This is rajas-driven giving. You make a temple, and you put your name on it. You give food for one thousand people and have your name called out, that this food was given by you. You like that. In the end you want something for yourself in exchange for giving. Remember, this is not the purest form of giving either.

Krishna now describes the **highest form of giving** which is motivated by neither ignorance, nor greed, nor ambition. The highest form of giving is giving to truth, to beauty, to love. It is giving in devotion, without wanting anything in return, giving all and everything without doubting. This is the highest form of giving in the sense of devotion, surrender and gratitude.

Sanchit karma is your accumulated karma from your past lives. It is like a bag, you do not know what you are holding. Giving is the only way you can affect it. You do not know what is next thing coming from the Sanchit karma, whether it is a cookie or a snake. But by just constantly giving to the right person or the right cause you can change what karma gets activated.

Prarabdha karma, which is karma ready to be experienced in this life, is difficult to deal with, and dhridha prarabdha karma, which is fixed karma ready to be experienced, is one of the most difficult karmas. It can be affected, and your society as a collective can be changed. There are societies who master it, and you never see them begging.

You never see a Sikh begging because they are masters of giving. They go and volunteer in their langars, the community kitchen or gurudwala and feed hundred thousand people every day. You never see a Sikh begging because they have taken care of their own karma as well as the social karma. They have developed a good support system. Because of that you never see a Sikh begging.

You never see a Jew begging either because they are the same with the giving. Highly educated people, strong people. They give, and they teach their strengths. An uncle and his nephew meet. The uncle mentors the nephew, passes on his skills, shares his ideas, shares his connections. When the nephew one day become an uncle he will do the same. There are funds which were started by somebody hundred years ago, and now all the children in the line of that family and their remote families enjoy the best education. Nobody is uneducated, nobody is poor, nobody is hungry. Why? Because somebody stood up and took care of the sanchit karma of the community and also took care of their own karma.

The wealthiest people ever, how did they become like that? By learning to give and share. What is the difference between someone with a royal spirit and someone with a spirit of poverty? Someone poor in spirit is unable to give whereas someone royal in spirit is able to give and share. The person poor in spirit is not able to give but is holding. That person is unable to be in gratitude, that is the poverty of the mind. So if you want to create wealth in your life, start giving and sharing. Give your time and work by volunteering. If you connect to animals, then volunteer taking care of animals. And the greatest of the giving is to the divine, for the divine.

Imagine the people who build the great universities like Nalanda, Takshashila, Vikramshila thousands of years ago. This is the highest form of giving. Some of the patrons who funded these universities were the kings in Bali, thousands of miles away from India. Even today it takes 11 hours by flight to reach there from India. The majority of the knowledge which reached Bali came from the ancient universities in India, especially Nalanda, and even today ancient rituals and education from those education centres are still alive there.

Karma can be mastered with meditation, and through devotion you have the blessings and power to face it. The path of jnana or self-enquiry teaches you to get disentangled from it, but there is only one thing that can change karma. The only thing that can change which karma will come to you, is giving. That is how important this element is.

This chapter guides you on connecting with the divine through faith, belief and worship. It guides you on connecting to food and connecting to your karma and karma of the society. This chapter can transform your life. If you have a difficult life, read this chapter and the chapter 5 and 6 on meditation. With these three chapters transform your life. And if you find meditation difficult, just read this chapter, day in and day out, read this and change your life. Gain mastery of these three core aspects of life; your belief which gives you meaning, your food which gives you life energy, and your giving which gives you power and mastery of your karma and social karma.

Now Krishna is advancing further. ***Om Tat Sat***. Invoke the divine with *Om*, with the power of *Om*. *Om* in itself is a whole meditation and pranayama. *Om*.

You can divide it, just practice the *Ma* part with humming. *Ma*. Make a meditation technique from it, invoking the divine. With *Om* you can invoke the divine. Put your hands on your heart and start humming. After 10 minutes let your hands rest on your knees.

Chant it in the short form or in the long form. Chant it in a divided form. Rest in the vibration of humming for half an hour, for 45 minutes, for one hour.

Master art of *Om* in your life, it is a key element.

If you remember Krishna, then *Hari Om*. Connect it with your breath. With every exhalation, let *Hari Om* be your mantra. *Hari Om*. Let this energy of *Om* guide you.

Hari is divine. *Hari* is the name of Vishnu. *Hari* is the name of Krishna. Invoke *Om* with the name of *Hari*. Just rest in the humming, in the vibration of *Om*.

My favourite has been humming for one hour, early morning, in the middle of the night. Wake up, set an alarm for two o'clock, do *Om* and go back to sleep. In the night, do only the humming part. Wake up in the morning, start with *Om*. Start the morning with that. *Om*. If your mind is agitated, too much of a monkey mind, do humming. Connect with *Om*, that is the key.

The second element is *Tat Sat,* and the whole as a mantra, *Om Tat Sat*. *Om* invokes the divine, *Tat* is, I offer this action.

Om Tat, I devote this action, this selfless action to the divine. And *Sat*, I will take this action to the end. I'm not going to stop in between, I'm not going to give up in between. I have decided, and I will take my action to the very end. And in the end I will say *Om Tat Sat*. This is yajña, give everything. *Om Tat Sat,* I invoke the divine and offer my action to the divine for the truth. *Sat* also means truth. Parabrahman is the only truth. Ishvara is the only truth. I offer my action to the divine for Ishvara. I invoke the *Om*. I offer it to the divine for Ishvara. I offer my meditation for the Paramātman, for Krishna, for Ishvara. That is *Om Tat Sat*.

Krishna gives you this divine mantra, a life changing mantra. This is a present. This is diamond. Now this mantra is so easily available, and people do not know the value of it because it is just there. You can read it everywhere, and it is part of the daily life. Understand the meaning of it, and connect with the meaning of it. You can transform your life with this mantra.

Hari Om Tat Sat. Om Tat Sat. Tat Sat. Hari Om Tat Sat. Tat Sat. To the divine for Krishna. For the truth. To the divine for the truth. *Tat*. All is divine. All is divine. Every aspect of your life is divine. *Hari Om Tat Sat.*

Chapter 18

Seeking the Core, Where the Truth Embraces

Chapter 18 is one of the most defining chapters of Bhagavad Gita. This knowledge, when rightly understood, can build your life and bring health, wealth, wisdom, prosperity, success, transcendence, devotion, joy and celebration. And not only to your life but to the life of loved ones as well. This is the chapter which can build civilisations, which can create a strong future for humanity.

If misunderstood, though, this chapter creates confusion. Or rather, your own ignorance projected upon this chapter can create confusion, doubt, and misunderstandings, which will not be good for your life. So, it is very important to read this chapter with care and diligence, to see and observe for yourself and know the complexity of this wisdom.

See this wisdom like a complex music with many instruments playing together and creating great music, or see it as many colours coming together and creating art, or as many ingredients in a dish coming together and creating an exquisite taste. Where exactly is this taste? This taste comes when many ingredients are in harmony. The same is in the nature. When all the nature elements are in harmony, life blossoms. On the planets where harmony of the nature elements is not there, life does not blossom, whereas on earth, the nature elements are in harmony. So everything is interconnected and interdependent and complete in itself. This chapter is about this **interconnectedness**, interdependence and completion.

Where is **beauty**? Beauty comes when many aspects different qualities, many different colours, many different fragrances, many different shapes, many different elements, many different structures, come together to create beauty. If you take things apart to see where exactly the beauty is, you can not find it. When you see a flower, where exactly is the beauty in the flower? No scientist can pinpoint it. But the insight could be there that all the colours are in harmony, all the shapes are in harmony, the nature of the flower is in harmony, the nature of the elements in the flower, the nature of the flow of prakṛti in that flower is in harmony, which leads to beauty. So this is complex.

The general understanding of this chapter has unfortunately become quite simplistic. Simple is beautiful, and beauty is in simplicity, but reducing something complex by ignoring important parts of it, without seeing the interconnectedness of the different parts, and without seeing the truth in its complexity, this is simplistic.

There is an ancient story, a Jain story from one of the Tirthankars. The

Jain community is one of the most hardworking and reliable, and 25% of India's taxes come from businesses run by Jain, who make up only 0.5% of the population. The ancient Jain scriptures contain much wisdom, and this story of 'the Blind Men and the Elephant' sums up the **complexity of truth**. In the story, five blind people come across an elephant for the first time. They each touch a different part of the big elephant, like the leg or the tail or the trunk, and by this they learn and imagine what the elephant is like. The blind men then describe the elephant to each other, each according to his own limited experience and imagination, and all the descriptions are different. In order to see the elephant, you need to have eyes, you need to have vision, to see, to know the whole complex nature of the elephant. The elephant is big, and so is truth.

These blind men were not lying when describing the elephant differently. They were seeing only one aspect of the truth, but if they start fighting over how the elephant is, the wise one would think, "are you guys stupid? You all are describing the elephant from your individual experience of touching different parts. No one has experienced the whole elephant."

Feeling the whole elephant would give a better picture than feeling only a part of it, but there are also other ways of experiencing it. If you have sight, you can see it, and if you have hearing, you can hear it. The same is with the truth. Truth is complex. It has many different aspects and can be experienced in many different ways.

Somebody claiming that a particular insight from the truth is the only insight would be fooling himself, and if he teaches that to others, it would also become a hindrance for others in understanding the complexity of the truth. So, do not limit yourself to identification with some interpretation or some insight. See the complex nature of the truth. See the complexity. Have simplicity and purity in your heart to see, understand, experience and live the complex nature of the truth.

Here, Krishna again points to the **interconnected paths to liberation**, saying, you are not limited by one particular idea or one particular path. Life is a pathless land, and it is a pathless path to the truth. All paths are interconnected, they are interdependent and one leads to the other.

If you totally surrender in devotion, and you see the beauty of courage, surrender, love and compassion in the devotion, then self-enquiry is bound to flower in you. Jnana, the knowingness, the is-ness, the zen, as they call it in Japan, is bound to flower in your being. And if your zen is successful, if your self-enquiry is successful, you are bound to be in love, you are bound to be in devotion. The gratitude will flower for your guru, for your master, for the divine nature of this existence. That is bound to happen. You are bound to devote your action, your daily life in selfless action in the service of the humanity, in the service of the divine, in the service of the future generations to come. And you are going to devote your action to the divine.

These ways or paths to liberation are interconnected. Your meditation is connected with your self-enquiry. If you are sincere, then self-enquiry is bound to blossom. If you are on the path of selfless action, sooner or later you are going to question, who am I? What is the nature of the reality? What is meaning in life? What is this life for? This is bound to happen. If your meditation blossoms, you will become sensitive and compassionate. That is going to take place. But if you start to think yourself superior to others because you meditate, this means your meditation is not blossoming, that is clear. So in this way, it is a test. If one path leads to another, it is a sign of flowering of that path.

Meditation in form of abhyas or discipline, self-enquiry, devotion, and selfless action with the core of flow, these paths are interconnected. Know thyself from it, know thyself. Develop vigour, vitality and energy from pranayama. Master pranayama, and master the senses with insight and understanding. Master the union of these paths in you.

Krishna then instructs to **be true to your nature**. If devotion is blossoming in you right now, and there is no call for self-enquiry, but you want to celebrate, be in love and devote your actions and your seva to the divine, then let that be. Do not impose that which is not happening naturally in you. Do not judge yourself for that. Let that be the case and be surrendered to how it is. Trust, trust. It takes time to make good wine. It takes maturity. This is a lifetime journey, so do not be hard on yourself by judging yourself, and thinking yourself limited to only one path. That is your nature, let it flower. Be authentic, that is Krishna's core message here. Be authentic, and be true to yourself. Do not fall into comparison, neither with other people nor with ideas of how it should be.

Beware of the **ambition of reaching**, making an ambition out of liberation. Liberation is not an ambition. If you plant a seed, and you water it well, the seed is bound to flower. That will surely happen. If the seed every day chants "flower, flower, flower, flower", that will not make the seed flower. So do not fall into the trap of making enlightenment and liberation into a goal and an ambition and then become greedy for it. That is a pitfall of the mind.

There are many different traditions of the Vaisnava tantra where the focus is on the interconnectedness, on the divine oneness of Purusha and Prakṛti. For example, interconnectedness of body and breath, interconnectedness of mind and body, and interconnectedness of heart and feelings. Here, one is aware of the interconnectedness, the attention is on the interconnectedness of the aspects rather than on only one of them.

Your attention could also be solely on devotion, if that is your nature, or it could be that you flow from self-enquiry to selfless action, or that you are committed diligently to only one path. There is freedom in this, but it should not come from ideas of how it should be.

Now Krishna makes us aware of **the gunas' effect on the inner path**.

Be aware of the **tamas nature** inside yourself. Beware of ignorance, self-righteousness, limiting ideas like "this is who I am", and reluctance to look outside that. You may be limited to your idea, ideology, conditionings, thought patterns, and habits, and be reluctant to look outside that. The first step is to come out of the limitedness because it confines you.

Around the world, many people think that their way of life is the best, and nothing better has ever happened. If their civilisation is economically advanced, the chance of having this illusion increases. Do not fall into that illusion. Great civilizations are not built by ignorance and limitedness. It takes vision, it takes clarity, it takes wisdom, it takes courage, and it takes generations of hard work to build great civilizations. So be aware of rigidity in yourself.

Be open. Have double up openness. Be open to different cultures, be open to different ways of looking at things. By being open, you are open about your rigidity, and that is the core. It is not that you need to completely change yourself to something else, which you are not, but by being open, you will not fall into the limitedness and rigidity of tamas.

What is the secret of India's ability to survive and thrive, despite being attacked for thousands of years in many different ways? Many other civilizations that experienced such attacks could not survive, but India not only survived, it thrived in every dimension. Of course it got its wound which it is still healing, but it is getting even stronger. The secret is that India is aware of the tamas nature of ignorance and rigidity. Other cultures that were rigid but unaware of their own rigidity let to destruction of many people, countries and nations. And the people who were limited in a certain sense could not take the shock of invasions and attacks.

If you can spot the tamas nature in yourself, like ignorance, rigidity, and limiting ideas, then you will be able to identify it in others also, and by this you can protect yourself from it.

Be aware that you are not limited to certain conditioned thought patterns. Be thorough in your research, be thorough in your wisdom, be thorough in your understanding. And through that thoroughness, through that depth, see and achieve clarity.

Now Krishna moves on to examine how the gunas affect or express themselves in our actions, will, happiness and intellect. The insight Krishna gives here is not meant for judging others, by which you would hurt your spirit, your soul, and your heart. Do not create judgments from this, but turn you attention inwards and see. Of course see it outwards also, but as a reflection, for you to be able to learn and pinpoint it in yourself. This wisdom is for your own understanding of how the gunas work.

First Krishna describes **how tamas unfolds in our actions**. Very often we are unaware of what motivates our actions, or we are unaware of the outcome our action will have. Instead, our immediate needs are at the centre. Krishna says, it is alright to pay attention to your needs and take care of them, but you must be aware of what motivates your action. You must know what is driving you and not allow your actions to rise out of lethargy, laziness, procrastination, ignorance, carelessness, negligence or even lack of motivation. Do not let these aspects of the tamas nature overpower you, especially complete lack of motivation. You are a human being, have motivation to win, to reach, to conquer.

In the past, in the history of India, many people who were in the tamas energy of negligence and lethargy wanted to reach straight away to sattva and then to liberation. No, that is not the way. You must develop strength. Remember that the rules of Kurukṣetra and Dharmakṣetra are different. They are not happening in a different place, it is exactly the same place. The same Arjuna is fighting in Kurukṣetra, where he is aiming to win, but the moment he is looking inward, his motivation is advancing the truth, advancing the inner force. His actions are devoted to the divine, yet he is in Kurukṣetra and strategically moving towards winning. But if you took away Arjuna's strength, if you took away Arjuna's focus, if you took away Krishna's strategy, and Arjuna just instantly wanted to devote his action, how would that be? He would not even have any action to devote. He would not have any motivation to devote.

The hopelessness and lack of drive and vision of the tamas state must be overcome. For that you must **develop inner strength** and a vision for your life. You must develop an inner ability to stand up for yourself and fight for what you believe in, and an ability to aim for it and work hard for it. If you are not even able to do that, then how would you be able to devote your action to the divine? You would not even have the will to take action and claim responsibility, neither would you have the courage to stand for your values. Most likely you would not be able to devote anything to the divine, because you would only have lethargy and confusion and hopelessness. Would you devote that to the divine?

Develop inner strength. Arjuna is strong, Arjuna is clear,

and Arjuna is ambitious. Arjuna wants to win. He has the motivation of the ego, and Krishna tells him to overcome it. Overcome it through sattva, guidance and meditation. Master it, but not at the cost of strength. Kurukṣetra is about winning, so win, Dharmakṣetra is about meaning, so find meaning. Devote the winning to the divine, devote not only your action, but its fruits, to the divine. Do the action, get the fruits and devote it to the divine, both.

This is what Arjuna is doing. His strength and his action is for the divine, his success is to the divine, his winning, the fruits of the battle is to the divine. Every aspect, from the beginning to the end is going to the divine. He has mastered the ambition and the ego through sattva.

Tamas without consciousness and love keeps you stuck in **comfort zone**. A comfort zone of thought, of mindset, of well trodden routines of life. You need to **come out of it through will**. If you do not have will you can develop it.

There are many different forms of will that one can develop, like the will to survive, the will to thrive or the will to excellence. Here, we will explore the **will to excellence**. If you are an entrepreneur, build a successful business for yourself, if you are a student, master the subject you are studying, if you are a musician, learn best of the music, and if you are a designer, learn from the masters and take the best education. Whatever skill you are learning, develop that skill to the best. If you make chai, make the best chai. If you clean floors, the floors should reflect the purity of your soul. If the floor is not clean and does not reflect your pure heart, then it is not right, because that floor is a reflection of who you are. Let the excellence reflect in your room, make it the cleanest, the finest, properly ordered and organised.

Some people find it easy to organise things outside, but

the inside is a mess. The self-esteem and self-respect are broken, they have constant self-doubts, there is a burden of unexpressed and repressed emotions, and the senses and the wit are dull. This is your inner room, let it shine in excellence. Develop wit, humour, courage and authenticity. Be authentic. Let your inner self reflect through your communication and expression. Put your inner room as well as your outer room in order.

With the foundation of will to excellence you can come out of the tamas energy that otherwise takes you towards hopelessness, fickleness, laziness and procrastination. You need to win over that force through will. You must overcome it and master it.

Krishna says that the nature of **tamas** also reflects in the **intellect and thought process.** It shows itself as self-righteousness, like "my way is the right way" and as constant self-doubts despite high qualifications and excellent work. The self-righteousness and self-doubt is how tamas shapes your thinking. Do not let such unconscious tamas affect you. If you really want tamas, have the best tamas in a good, deep, and restful sleep. That is the moment to go fully into tamas. Tamas should not enter your life in form of lethargy or laziness. You may be a very active person, thinking yourself far from lazy, but whenever your intellect gets challenged, you tend to escape. You do not want to think, but prefer to be given a simplistic idea and run with that without questioning it, so you can continue to just do, do, do, do, do, do. That is **intellectual laziness** or lethargy.

Unconscious tamas also reflects on your **emotional state**. You may be scared of feelings and emotions, living in a very cold culture where you have to hide your emotions and feelings and are unable to feel or express any of them.

Or you may lack emotional hygiene. From outside you appear well dressed and fashionable, but inside you are a total mess, a broken human being who can break completely with any intense storm of emotion. Grief can break you, sorrow can break you, any loss in your life can break you.

Or you are just stuck in loneliness and isolation. The modern day metropolis is full of such people, living in box shaped apartments, lonely and isolated on their phones without anything meaningful in life. This is modern day slavery. Do not fall into this modern day slave mindset, into loneliness and isolation.

Come out of the unconscious tamas. **Rise above it through sattva**, through developing a vision for yourself.

Write down your vision. For example, how do you see your life in 5 years, in 3 years? If you want to change, if you want to achieve something, then make that into your vision, make that into your goal.

Set a strategy for how to reach your goal. Which actions will make you reach? Which small 5-10 minutes actions could propel you forward? If you want to study something, start studying it for 10 - 20 minutes. Then slowly increase it to 1 hour every day. I can promise you, if you practice playing a music instrument 1 hour every day, in 1 year you would be at least at the intermediate state. If you exercise half an hour every day, then by the end of the year you would see what a transformation has happened with your body, and your self-respect would grow from that. This is the power of small changes if you keep the consistency. Direction of sattva and consistency of tamas.

Even if you climb the greatest mountains, it is through small steps. Many mountaineers have had the dream of climbing all the 14 peaks of 8000 meters. Some of them achieved it.

How? With a clear vision, a strict time frame and taking one step at a time, consistently and persistently.

Set a time frame for your actions and goals and stick to it. In the previous chapter we heard Krishna saying, *Om Tat Sat*. *Sat* means end, finish, you have reached, O*m* is invoking the divine and t*at* means to the divine. You are devoting the end of whatever action you complete to the divine, saying O*m Tat Sat*. Giving yourself a time frame for finishing your task is very helpful. But be humble when setting a time frame, know your limitations. Do not be so arrogant in your ambition that you break on under the load or you end up with too much work and completely give up.

Krishna guides you to first **come out of the crooked tamas state**, where tamas lacks consciousness and love and is not in harmony with the other gunas. Tamas does have its place, in sleep and in other aspects of life, because from the darkness, from the seed state, the flower will blossom.

Some of the worst losers are very arrogant, while some of the most successful people are very humble. This is not a coincidence as the ignorance of unconscious tamas brings arrogance. In this kind of ignorance, you are careless. You are unaware of your motivation to act as you do. Forget about purpose and meaning, you are not even aware how you shape your life. The awareness of what you want in life, what you are aiming for is lacking.

The challenge of unconscious tamas can be present in different aspects of life. Someone may have sorted out their work and career and overcome the heavy tamas energy there, but when it comes to relating they may be not giving it proper time, may be lethargic or have an arrogant attitude. Or they be emotionally unhygienic, meaning that they are careless with own and others emotional space, like spreading irritation or negativity around. So one is not necessarily stuck in tamas in all areas of life.

Krishna then talks about the next stage, **rajas guna**. Once the hurdle of unconscious and unharmonious tamas has been overcome, you may face the challenges of rajas, like impulsivity, attachment and too much goal orientation.

You may struggle with impulsivity, letting your mood and emotions decide the direction you go.

Another pitfall of rajas is to become arrogant when achieving success. If you are winning, remember that your winning is not only due to your effort. Factors like blessings, good luck, the country you are in, and your family and friends supporting you play a major role. Do not think all the success in your life is only because of you, and any failure is because of others. When somebody else is successful you think that the success is due to the circumstances, but when you are successful, it is because of you. Do not fall into this trap of ego.

Another trap of rajas is becoming overly focused on the goal or the reward, trying so hard to achieve and win that you miss the journey. And if you lose or are unable to achieve your goal, you lose all hope and may go further down into a negative spiral of self doubts and victimhood.

When you fail, be aware that failure is not the end. Every failure is a learning lesson. Move on, do not lose hope. Continue.

Krishna points out that you have to **overcome the challenges of rajas**. Of course rajas brings a lot of passion, ambition, drive and motivation, but if you are in the battlefield, you will also face fear and doubt.

You need to overcome self-doubt. The more competent you become, the more you will doubt yourself. This phenomenon is called the Dunning-Kruger effect, and the psychologist who coined this term won a Nobel prize for it. When some of the brightest scientists speak, they consider many possibilities at the same time, seeing the matter from several points, so they often do not appear very confident. On the other hand, someone new to the field can be very confident about their own abilities and knowledge because they do not yet know their own limits. The better you get in something, the more doubts will come. This is a sign that you are advancing, so do not be limited by doubt.

Sometimes rajas causes you to become biased, attached to your own opinion or view, and unable to see the reality as it is. You see your opinion or your way as the only one and are unable to see other perspectives, unable to see things objectively. Be aware of biases in yourself. The mind has many cognitive biases, and tends to take thinking shortcuts, which you must be aware of.

Do not be limited by fear, but develop courage. Develop mastery of intellect to challenge ideas. This is the beauty of the rajas energy, that it will take you to this dimension.

Mastery of rajas gives you a natural ability to collaborate and compete. When you are in Kurukṣetra, it is important to understand the kind of field you are in, whether it is a battle field or a playing field, whether the strategy and action is win-win, win-lose, or lose-lose. For example, Krishna and Arjuna are in the win-win part of Kurkshetra, whereas Karan and Arjuna are in the win-lose part of Kurukṣetra, where one will win and one will lose.

Throughout India's history many outsiders divided us and made us fight and compete with each other. We thought we were winning from each other because it appeared like that, but actually nobody was winning—everyone was losing. The energies were drained out, and somebody else from outside was winning. A third party was winning. A third party who was not even participating. This third party put us in the fight against each other, and sadly, even after 75 years of independence, the education system is still busy with it.

Krishna is making Arjuna understand the different **strategies of Kurukṣetra**. He is a master of the Kurukṣetra. He understands Kurukṣetra by heart. He understands the motivations of the different parties and how they move. If you do this, then the other party will do that. Sometimes Krishna tells Arjuna to attack, and Arjuna says, "yes, but". There is no but, no space for hesitation. When we are in Kurukṣetra, we need to advance, we need to move. The other is moving, and we need to answer it.

The rules depend on which part of Kurukṣetra you are in, whether you are in the collaborative or the competitive part. You should not be competing when you are in the collaborative part of Kurukṣetra, nor the other way around. Imagine if the Pandavas start to compete with each other. That would not work, and they would loose.

Develop a **good collaborative system**, where you support your team and collaborate with your community. Every member of the community should take care of the whole community, and the whole community should take care of each member.

Competition is important, as some forms of competition help you to grow. The ancient Vedantic dialogue or the Socratic dialogue is one of the finest form of dialogue, which leads to truth. This works is by collaborating and challenging each other at the same time. The core is for the truth, and wherever the truth starts to open and reveal itself, the other party stops and says, "wow, this is interesting". So it is a dialogue going towards the truth. Socratic and Vedantic dialogue is a good example of collaborating and challenging each other in order to reach. A competition which is challenging to each other, which is making each other strong, is a healthy competition whereas a competition which is making the other weak is not a good competition.

There are challenges or **hindrances of rajas** which must be overcome, like possessiveness, over-attachment to ideas, to relations, to where you live, to what you do. Be aware of these attachments. Too much focus on goals, too much focus on the reward and working only for that is another challenge. Being influenced by different emotions like fear, greed, possessiveness, attachment, or stinginess. Absence of consciousness in rajas brings these challenges, and they must be attended and overcome.

Krishna indicates that some of the challenges of the gunas can destroy your life and the life of others around you, and if allowed growth, by which the scale increases, they can become a hindrance to the growth of the humanity. The way you can be aware of this is by being aware of it in yourself. If one is aware of these challenges in oneself, one is aware of it in the world.

Now Krishna moves on to explain the **different types of happiness that the gunas bring**.

Sometimes the carelessness of **tamas brings a superficial, momentary happiness** which will change into sorrow. You are careless about your time, you are careless about your money, you are careless about your life, you are careless about your job, your action, your family. That carelessness can bring a certain tiny happiness, which is actually a short-lived relief resulting from avoidance of the necessary in order to continue in whatever inertia is there already. This type of superficial happiness from carelessness destroys your life. The carelessness come from ignorance. You are reluctant to look see the truth and look into the issues in your life, you do not want to read the scriptures, and you do not want to read this. This is carelessness. But the care and diligence you will put into reading, the heartfulness you will put into reading and educating yourself will transform your life.

Rajas brings a certain happiness which comes from indulging in pleasures and moving from one pleasure to another, from one happiness to another. The happiness which come from possessing things, the happiness which come from rewards and profits or the fruits of the action. That is a certain form of happiness. It is better than the superficial and momentary happiness which tamas brings, but it is still a very limited form of happiness, and it will limit your life.

There is so much energy which goes into holding on to and possessing things, into projections, possessions, jealousy, and comparison. This takes so much energy that you do not have any energy available for love. Krishna says, go beyond attachment. Drop the possessiveness and control and reach to true love. Love and take care. If you stop being attached, your relations will not break. No, your relations will be even more beautiful, as you have more energy available to pay attention and to be deeply be in love.

Non-attachment or **beyond attachment** does not mean that you become cold, as in detached. That is not what Krishna is saying. He is pointing to what your core motivation is, whether your core motivation is love or possessiveness, whether your core motivation is owning and controlling or it is giving and sharing. This is the difference between attachment and beyond attachment. Beyond attachment is not being cold, insensitive and arrogant, looking down on people who have relations, looking down on people who have families, being arrogant on your so-called path of meditation, seeing your partner as a hindrance in your meditation success and your work as a problem in your life. That is completely bullshit. Periodical renunciation from the daily humdrum is important, going away and coming back, that is part of life. But if you start to dim your senses and start to run away from the joys of life, from the simple happiness of life, and you try to escape that and go into cowardice, then that is not what Krishna advices.

What is sattva? Sattva is vision, and sattva is mastery, like mastering senses to the best, so they do not master you. You become master of desire, you become master of your action. You are able to devote your action, and you devote your every thought, every feeling to the divine.

From this, knowingness will manifest. And in this knowingness, you will see the impermanence, yet you will see the permanence of Ātman, of is-ness, of knowingness, that which is there, that which was, that which is, and that which would always be. You would be aware of the impermanence, of everything moving, moving, moving, changing, changing, changing, everything passing, passing. Young becoming old, old going to death, death becoming birth. You will see this.

Your motivation would be deep. You would be motivated by meaning, you would be motivated by love, by compassion, by taking the humanity forward, by transcendence, taking your consciousness from limited to infinite, going from darkness to light, moving from limited motivation to infinite motivation.

This is what sattva can bring in your life. You would be

full of vitality and vigour. Your senses would not be dull or repressed, but full of vitality and vigour. You would be upright and holding your values, and not only holding your values, but expressing and asserting them, as Krishna and Arjuna are doing. They are expressing their values through Bhagavad Gita. Because Krishna and Arjuna are expressing and asserting their values of truth, of beauty, of love, of compassion, of transcendence, this book became a friend to so many people, generations after generations. Bhagavad Gita became a friend to so many generations.

Krishna and Arjuna are asserting and expressing their values by fighting the battle with the Kauravas, because if they do not fight the battle, the ego of Duryodhana will win. Duryodhana is asserting his ego. He is asserting, "I want more". He wants not only the fruits of his own action but the fruits of everybody's action. Imagine the kind of kingdom which would have been there if Duryodhanas's ego had been allowed to continue asserting itself. Slavery would have come to such a kingdom, poverty would come to such a kingdom, suppression would come, and exploitation would come.

Reach to the divine. You are divine, divinity is your right. Reach to the divine.

Call Krishna in your life. And when you call Krishna, when the divine starts manifesting in your life, when Ishvara principle start manifesting in your life, then the self in form of 'poor me to whom life is happening' will start to disappear. Excuses like "I'm born in a poor family, I am weak, I cannot" will disappear. You will start to take charge of your life and become a leader of your life. When you take control of your life, when you master your life, when you master your will and your senses, then life is no longer just happening to you.

Build success in your life. Come out of poverty, ill health and misfortune. Learn to devote yourself to the divine, and you will find a deeper meaning in life. Give your action and your success to the divine.

Through this, a transformation will come in your consciousness, and you will see the non-duality. You will see that all is divine, I am divine, you are divine. All was divine, all is divine, all will be divine and there is nothing but divine.

Krishna is giving you this vision, the highest vision. He is showing you the path and helping you as a friend, walking along with you. What other guru would do that? This is the greatest guru who ever walked on this earth, who has chosen to become a charioteer for Arjuna. Imagine the compassion. He is not standing on the platform, shouting from there or shouting from the mountaintop or from a cave. He is coming along with you, becoming your driver, as it would be in the modern times, and guiding you through the chaos of life. This is the great guru Krishna, the true Adi Guru Krishna, the ancient guru Krishna, the sadhu guru Krishna. The immense wisdom is coming in form of compassion, in form of friendship.

Krishna is an inspiration, guiding you on every aspects of life. Even psychological challenges which you will face on the inner journey, he is telling you about that. He could have just said, this is the path Arjuna, walk. These are the meditation techniques, practice. He could have just said that, but no, he is coming along with you. He got down from his throne and is going along with you and guiding you. This is the power of Krishna, this is the power of the Ishvara principle.

Krishna says, it is important to **understand renunciation**. If the ignorant mind says, renounce the action, do not follow that. Imagine if the sun stopped doing, what would happen? If even for a single day the sun stopped doing, what would happen? So Krishna says, do not drop the action. If you want to renounce, if you are on to the dropping journey, then drop the doer. Drop your greed for the fruit of your action and find meaning in the action itself through divine. Make the process of the action complete in itself, so every moment of the action is complete, so every element of the action is complete.

Krishna explains that **dropping the fruit of the action** does not mean that you do not fight for your rights, that you do not fight for the result of your action in the world. Krishna and Arjuna are fighting for the land that belongs to them. They are fighting for their people. What Krishna means is to drop the inner attachment. If you must be attached, then be attached to the meaning, be attached to Krishna, be attached to the divine.

Do your action and get the best reward. Create success for yourself, for your family, for your nation, for your country, for the humanity. Develop the best technologies, master the best skills, develop the deepest wisdom. Know what kind of Kurukṣetra you are in. If you are in a Kurukṣetra of making profit, then make the best profit in an ethical and sustainable way, while taking care of your people. If you are in the battlefield, then win. That is the rule of battle.

In this process also **be aware who you are**. Who are you? Ask yourself this deep question. And be aware what kind of self you are creating. The doer is happening. Do not be in illusion that straight from ignorant tamas you would become enlightened. You will face the kartabhav or doer, the drishtabhav or observer, and the bhoktabhav or experiencer in yourself. These are different bhavs or self feelings you will go through. Be aware how this self is developing. Are you moved by Instagram likes? Are you moved by name and fame? Are you moved by what people think about you? Are you moved by your success and failure? That is a self you are constructing. Be aware of that internal process, what kind of karta or doer is developing in you, what kind of bhokta or experiencer is developing.

Do not just say, "I am Ātman". That is the biggest illusion and a great pitfall. Greedy so-called Vedanta learners come to India from all over the world and fall straight into the trap of "I am that". They end up having a poor life, poverty stricken, but with the arrogance of "I am Ātman". You are not aware yet. You are not even aware of your ego, of how your ego is formed. You are not aware of your self and how it is developing. When you are not aware of the very foundation, then how would you be aware of Ātman?

So, do not think that you can jump straight from ignorant tamas to enlightenment and skip the rajas in between. Some of the best art and culture is created by people with very powerful rajas. Some of the greatest successes have been achieved by people with strong rajas. So, be aware of the nature of rajas.

See how the self is developing in you. Is it developing as a poor me, a victim of life, full of self-doubt? Or are you developing a good pride for who you are, self-respect, self-esteem, pride of your language and culture, and pride of the effort you put into your action? I am not saying that you should own it, possess it, and get biased towards it, that would be challenges of rajas, which must be overcome. But do develop self-respect, respect for the clothes you wear and for what you represent.

Krishna is a pioneer of his time. He is bringing this great ancient wisdom that even today it is the finest wisdom.

This pioneering knowledge he is bringing for us, for you. Bhagavad Gita is a great work of psychology, sociology, philosophy, science, art, and spirituality. Know that, and carry this book with pride, that "this is my Bhagavad Gita. This is the knowledge which is helping me transcend to the divine." Then of course dedicate it to the divine. Because who are you, and what is yours? This dedication to the divine is the highest. Find meaning in that. But do not skip the first part, the important part. Do not be such a hypocrite thinking that you would straight away go from ignorance to enlightenment. That will not happen.

Be humble, be humble, be humble. You are going to fall many times, you are going to do many mistakes. Do not judge yourself.

And be diligently aware that your actions are not hurting others. Socrates was poisoned, and his words to the people who gave him poison were, "I am going to overcome this body, I will change this body to a new one." But could they change their soul? They would have to live with their soul, their karma, life after life.

Now Krishna moves on to make us **understand liberation** or enlightenment. The liberation has its own nature. In one of the ancient talks, Buddha says that a master is one who is compassionate. An enlightened being who is not sharing, the enlightenment is there, but the sharing brings a a different fragrance to enlightenment. It is fertile, it is potent, and it can bring others to enlightenment.

Krishna says, know that this wisdom is unique. Do not throw pearls to the pigs, know whom you share it with, but do share it. Learn to share this wisdom with others. This wisdom can bring transformation to the lives of others, that is what Krishna is highlighting. If you learn to give now, then when the full liberation is coming to you, you will be giving and can thus become a guide to the thousands on the inner path.

Krishna then elucidates **our inherent nature**. He says, our inherent nature is fluid. It is not a static and stagnant process. It is a moving and evolving process. We can see it in our daily life, in how we make our living, in what actions which we do, and in what kind of nature or guna is there. Be aware of this nature. See this nature as an evolving phenomenon, something that can be learned, something that can grow and evolve. It is something which you can take pride in. By pride is meant respect, not ego, but the respect you develop for this.

Krishna says that our heart seeks courage, our mind or knowingness seeks clarity, our senses seeks fulfillment, and our needs seek food, shelter and human connection. Everything in this universe is giving us and serving us. This is the heart of Krishna's message.

Krishna explains **how the gunas manifest in our motivations**. Some people are motivated mainly by having their needs fulfilled. They do a job, and through the payment from the job their needs are fulfilled. They live from paycheck to paycheck. Krishna defines that as a state, a foundational state, which is important. Maybe your nature is like that, and you have no interest in looking beyond. That is perfectly fine, Krishna says, just stick to that. But the action you do for fulfilling the needs, devote this action for the divine. Do bhajan or singing devotional songs, bhojan or serving food, and seva or service for the divine. If you do not want to think more than that, it is perfectly fine. This is Krishna's message.

Gangotri is the origin of the river Ganga from where she flows to the ocean. It is the same Ganga all the way to the ocean. One cannot say that Ganga in the Gangotri is the superior

Ganga, or Ganga reaching the ocean is less of a Ganga. That is not what Krishna is saying. It is the same Ganga all the way, Krishna says. Respect it as the same Ganga.

Today you are motivated by needs, but maybe tomorrow your needs would be fulfilled and you will aim for understanding sensual pleasures, wanting to nurture and take care of the senses and to enjoy the pleasure and happiness in life. Or maybe your motivations are not limited to needs but more of rajas type, focused on profiteering, reaching and trading. Commerce is very important to you. You want to farm and store the goods and you are thinking ahead. You are not just thinking of the immediate needs of this week, this month, but you are thinking two years ahead, three years ahead. You are investing your money, and you are taking good care of your people. It is not only your needs, but you are aware of the needs of the others, you are aware of the needs of the people who are working with you, for you. Your horizon become bigger. If this is your nature, let it be your nature, Krishna says. Master it.

Remember Ganga, she is the same Ganga no matter where you meet her. If you cut Ganga somewhere, the whole part of the land would become dry, and famine would come. She is the same Ganga whether coming from Gangotri or reaching different parts of the land.

If you are going through the stage of rajas in your life, devote your profit, devote every aspect of your life, your happiness, your pleasures, your joys, and your transactions for the divine. Whatever you do, give it for the divine. Make it into a selfless action. Let your money serve the divine. Build great universities, build great temples of devotion, build great ashrams where people can learn and study, and do yoga and meditation, where people can gather, and great teachings can manifest. So devote your profit, devote your money, devote your resources which you generated from farming, or which the commerce has given you from your investment. The money which has come, devote that money in the service of the divine. The flow of the Ganga reaches, Krishna says.

When the gunas are in harmony, your motivation is deeper than the tamsic motivation of security and fulfilment of needs or just the rajas motivation of profit or pleasure of senses. There is a deep meaning in your life. Meaning and purpose, sattva is your main motivation of life. You are ready to face the battles of life. You have courage, and you are ready to lead and motivate others. You are ready to motivate people around, a whole community or a nation for the better, for innovation, for advancement of the civilisation. And you are able to protect and guard this great culture. You are able to take responsibility for now as well as for the future generations. You stand tall with courage and you have this inner power to motivate people. When they are feeling low on energy, you are able to bring them hope, vitality and courage. You are able to fight for purpose, for meaning, for cause and devote your winning, devote your strength, your courage to that. You are able to advance to the new. If you are in technology advancing the technology to new, not just establishing trade, but advancing, like taking a landline phone to a smartphone. That advancement is your motivation. You are ready to fail, not one time but ten times, hundred times. You are ready to challenge the ideas that are limiting you, your community or your nation. If that is your nature, then be true to that nature and devote it to the divine. Make it into a selfless act and let that be your path.

Harmony and awakening of the gunas brings compassion for humanity, hence you are moved by compassion and devotion. The clarity of vision comes with which you are able to see the path others cannot see. You are able to see details that can change the life for others. You can impart this knowledge, those skills to others and empower them through that. You are dedicated to your values, express them, and stay true to them. You hold those values for the humanity, for the civilization. You develop a clarity of insight, a clarity of wisdom, you develop a clarity of compassion, depth of compassion, depth of love. You become light, not only to yourself but light to the others. You stand with that clarity in yourself. If that is your nature, let it be your nature.

If Krishna were present in today's world, his guidance for Bharat today would be, that this is the land of devas and deva rishis. And his guidance to you who is from this blessed land would be **multi dimensional growth**.

Learn the art selfless action. Serve with dedication and sense of duty and responsibility, and give your best in every action. Educate yourself with useful knowledge, and equip yourself with skills and the strength of hard work.

Learn to grow your own food. Learn the art of trade and commerce. Learn to invest, learn to vision, learn to lead, learn to allocate and delegate tasks. Master the art of success.

Develop courage and a deep sense of responsibility. Be the person on whom others can rely, not only in times of happiness, but in times of distress and chaos as well.

Develop strength and integrity. Develop great insights. Learn the ancient wisdom. Be a guide to others, a light in the darkness, not only to your family and your friends, but to the humanity. Be that person.

Develop all of these qualities. Then you can stand tall and say that you have the clarity of the wise, you have the courage of the brave, you have honesty and integrity of values, you are able to serve, you are able to give every aspect of your service for the divine, for the humanity, for truth and love. You are able to stand tall and be upright with these values.

That is Krishna's message, and with this message, Krishna says, act, oh Arjuna, act. **Now is the time to act**. The enemies are at the door. Rise up and let us go to battle. Arjuna answers, all my doubts are finished. I am up. We are winning this battle.

And that is exactly what happened. Krishna and Arjuna won the battle, and because they won, we have Bhagavad Gita today. So, win your battles in life. Do not shy away from your battles. Do not shy away from action. When the call of action comes to you, take the call. Rise up. Rise for the truth, for love and for beauty.

Satyam Shivam Sundaram
Sat Chit Anand, Sat Chit Anand, Sat Chit Anand.
Hari Om Tat Sat